Pilgrim
Walk BY THE SEA

SUSANNE HASSELL *photographs by Paul Hassell*

Published by Vision Run Publishing
305 Portsmouth Rd. • Knoxville TN 37909
www.VisionRun.com

Copyright © 2014 by Susanne V. Hassell, www.HolyPaths.org

ISBN 978-0-9905081-0-6

Printed in the United States.
Printed on recycled paper.

Photography by Paul Hassell, www.PaulHassell.com

Design by Deb Hardison, www.DebHardison.com

DEDICATION

We dedicate this book to Sarah Elizabeth Hassell Carmichael, beloved daughter and sister.

SINCE YOU FIRST TODDLED INTO THE LAPPING WAVES AND TRIED TO SHOVEL ALL THE SAND ON THE BEACH INTO YOUR BRIGHT PINK BUCKET, YOU HAVE SHOWN A DEEP APPRECIATION OF THE SEA AND A DESIRE TO GRASP ALL THAT LIFE HAS TO OFFER.

MAY YOU BE FILLED WITH ALL GOD HAS PREPARED FOR YOU, KNOWING THAT THE MYSTERIES OF GOD ARE HIGHER THAN THE HEAVENS, DEEPER THAN THE GRAVE, LONGER THAN THE EARTH AND WIDER THAN THE SEA.

FROM JOB 11:7-9 NIV

ACKNOWLEDGMENTS

We are grateful to our walking companions, both on the trails and on our life journeys. Many helped to birth this book and we are especially thankful for our enthusiastic team:

Debbie Patrick and Barbara Jones, Vision Run publishers, for their tireless efforts, persevering even after the death of their father, George Patrick;

Deb Hardison, gifted graphic designer, who took simple words and photos and created something new and beautiful;

Georganne Shultz Hassell, Frances Slatery Cowan, and Lisa Murray, perceptive editors, who lovingly corrected far more than spelling and punctuation;

Rebecca Ramsey McDonald, who tenaciously sought copyright permissions.

Many others contributed with a story, an idea, a prayer, a beach house, or a collection of sea glass and shells. These include: Amanda Arwe, Mary Sue Bjorklund, David Gayk, Martha Ann Fulk, Nancy Vanzant Goodrum, Debbie Henn, Emily Huff, Eileen Judice, Dorothy Krieg, Jeanne Maxwell, Betty Skinner, Cary Slatery, and Jennifer Smith.

We extend our gratitude for the generosity of many authors whose creative wisdom found its way into the pages of this book. Just as it takes infinite grains of sand to create a beach, the influence of many contributors created a beautiful book.

HOW TO USE THIS FIELD GUIDE

On a pilgrimage to the Iona community, off the coast of Scotland, I was invited to take a day-long Pilgrim Walk around the island. I loved everything about that day: hiking outdoors with new friends from around the world, reading poetry and scripture, learning songs and history about the islanders.

As a retreat leader, I began to offer afternoon contemplative prayer walks and some people confided that the walk was the first time they had ever "really prayed." Prayer is an intimate conversation, speaking and listening to the One who loves us, but many have difficulty sitting in meditation. Quiet walking and attentive listening, however, enable us to pray in new ways as God speaks in the music of creation.

We learn as children to pray with our heads bowed, hands folded, and eyes closed. Though this posture shows reverence and helps us to focus on God, there are other ways to pray. Try praying today with your eyes, ears, and heart wide open. Absorb the colorful beauty before you. Hear the pounding waves and cries of gulls. Feel the wind and the gritty sand. Smell the salty air.

This way of praying enriches our journey as "pilgrims" with fresh eyes and ears to experience the holy in the ordinary. Most religions consider pilgrimage a significant spiritual discipline when we choose to be pilgrims, not just ordinary tourists. We can allow God to transform our sacred imagination, intentionally seeking the holy within and around us or we can hurry through life without being fully engaged, snapping photos of sacred sites and people along the way.

"The object of pilgrimage is not rest and recreation—to get away from it all. To set out on a pilgrimage is to throw down a challenge to everyday life … Pilgrimage is the kind of journeying that marks the move from mindless to mindful, soulless to soulful travel," explains Huston Smith, professor of Religious Studies at University of California at Berkley.

Pilgrimages spring from a deep yearning to encounter God, drawing us to special times and places where we cross the threshold into new, liminal space. Ancient travelers did not set out on pilgrimage casually because they understood that encounters with the unknown could change them.

Early Christian Celts described special places where they encountered God as "thin places." Only a thin veil separated the seen and the unseen, the natural world and the holy, the finite and the infinite, the physical and the spiritual realms. Be attentive to your own "thin places" as you walk this journey.

This is a field guide for your spiritual journey. Don't let it gather dust on your coffee table or nightstand. Use it. To experience God in nature, you must be in nature. If you cannot walk or if you have no access to the sea, the photographs will aid in your reflections.

Your whole universe, O God, O Creator, is a burning bush. It calls us to turn aside, to pay attention, To see and hear and sense— and to wonder and to praise, Grant us new eyes, new ears, and newly awakened hearts; To enter into your courts of nature And praise your holy presence here.

-Elizabeth Dodson Gray

TIPS FOR THE JOURNEY

As has been said, the point of traveling is not to arrive but to return home laden with pollen you shall work up into honey the mind feeds on.

-R. S. Thomas

If you are walking with a group, focus your eyes on the beauty around you, not on the one who is reading. The guide can stop anywhere along the way to read or pray, but all pilgrim walkers should feel the freedom to interact, stopping the group when they encounter something of interest.

Reflections can be found using the Index at the back or the titles on each page, arranged alphabetically by sea specimen or character quality: Awe, Balance, Boat, Broken Seashells, etc.

Pay attention. Be open to mystery.

Travel lightly with few possessions. Less is more.

Carry a journal and stop often to reflect. Jot down impressions, thoughts, feelings, and discoveries.

Immerse your journey in prayer. Speak and listen to God.

Walk leisurely, at a pace that suits you. The goal is not to "finish" the path, but to absorb the wonders of God that are before you.

If you must use words while you walk, speak softly. Express gratitude for all you experience.

Be mindful—fully present. Let go of your worries, unfinished tasks, and responsibilities for awhile. Too often, we focus on the past or the future. Receive the gift of Now. Thich Nhat Hanh recommends walking with no particular aim, just for the sake of walking. He instructs pilgrims to be aware of their breathing, not controlling it, but counting inhales and exhales as a means of mindful meditation.

Return with a tangible memento as a reminder of your experience: a shell, stone, feather, photograph, or poem; something that will remind you in the days ahead of what you have seen and heard.

Be gentle with yourself. Slow down. Rest. Be still and know God.

When we first arrive at a beach house, we throw open the windows and doors to let in fresh air. In the same way, our hearts need to be opened in order to breathe in God's Spirit:

Open wide the window of our spirits, O Lord, and fill us full of light;
Open wide the door of our hearts,
that we may receive and entertain you with all our powers of adoration and praise.

-Christina Rossetti

SUSANNE HASSELL

 usanne is founder and director of Holy Paths, Inc.
She has years of experience walking with people on their
faith journeys as a spiritual director and retreat leader.
She received a Masters in Child and Family Studies from the
University of Tennessee and founded three preschools in the
southeast. She completed the Certificate of Spiritual Formation
at Columbia Theological Seminary in Atlanta and a Masters in
the Art of Spiritual Direction and a Doctor of Ministry from San
Francisco Theological Seminary.

Susanne is the mother of three grown children: Jonathan,
Sarah, and Paul. She is committed to offering hospitality
and fostering unity, cooperation, and love within the church
community and others who seek to know God. Raised in
Jacksonville, FL, Susanne spent countless hours exploring ocean
treasures on the east coast. She now resides in Knoxville, TN
where she authored *Pilgrim Walk in the Woods* (2011) and enjoys
hiking in the Smoky Mountains.

PAUL HASSELL

Paul Hassell isn't strictly a photographer. Paul is in the light business.

An entrepreneur since the age of fifteen, a lover of solitude, and a loyal friend, Paul defies convention at every turn. You'll walk away from talking photography with him, and you'll have the sense that Paul is doing what he was created to do. This at-home-ness in himself and his craft becomes a kind of permission for others to find their vocations and live them.

Paul found what makes him tick and organized his life around that calling. He designed his own major at The University of TN: Freelance Photography and Writing for the Natural Environment. That's a mouthful. He's a member of NANPA, (North American Nature Photography Association) SANP, (Southern Appalachian Nature Photographers) and the NSA, (National Speakers Association) but the credentials matter less to him than sharing the profound experience. He points the way to a bigger truth and deeper reality.

Paul is the proud owner of Light Finds, Inc. Paul has been published in *National Parks Magazine, Time/Life, Nature's Best,* and National Geographic books. Learn more at http://www.LightFinds.us

Standing before powerful ocean waves, marvel that the Creator of such magnificent natural wonders desires an intimate relationship with you.

AWE

WHEN ISRAEL CAME OUT OF
EGYPT,
    THE HOUSE OF JACOB FROM A
PEOPLE
OF FOREIGN TONGUE,
JUDAH BECAME GOD'S SANCTUARY,
ISRAEL HIS DOMINION.
THE SEA LOOKED AND FLED,
THE JORDAN TURNED BACK...
TREMBLE, O EARTH, AT THE PRESENCE
OF THE LORD,
    AT THE PRESENCE OF THE GOD
OF JACOB,
WHO TURNED THE ROCK INTO A POOL,
    THE HARD ROCK INTO SPRINGS
OF WATER.

PSALM 114 NIV

The psalmist recounts the remarkable
deliverance of the Israelites from slavery
in Egypt. The exodus story includes the
miraculous crossing of the Red Sea and
the Jordan River. Mount Sinai shook in
God's presence as Moses received the
law. But perhaps the greatest miracle
here is that Earth is God's "sanctuary,"
that we live under God's "dominion."
To "tremble" at God's presence is to
recognize God's power and authority
over all creation and our human frailty
by comparison.

BALANCE

JESUS WENT OUT TO A MOUNTAINSIDE TO PRAY,
AND SPENT THE NIGHT PRAYING TO GOD.
WHEN MORNING CAME, HE CALLED HIS DISCIPLES
TO HIM AND CHOSE TWELVE OF THEM, WHO HE ALSO
DESIGNATED APOSTLES ... HE WENT DOWN WITH
THEM ... AND A GREAT NUMBER OF PEOPLE FROM ALL
OVER JUDEA ... HAD COME TO HEAR HIM AND TO BE
HEALED OF THEIR DISEASES.

LUKE 6:12-13, 17-18 NIV

So often in ministry, we try to do things ourselves.
If that doesn't work, we recruit a community to help.
If that fails, we remember to withdraw and pray. But
Jesus' example teaches the reverse order. Solitude is
being alone and quiet enough to hear God's voice
call you "beloved." There are many loud, competing
voices in our culture demanding proof that you are
loved, worthy, and relevant, but the assurance of
God's love brings freedom from such impossible
challenges.

After Jesus prayed alone all night, he chose twelve
disciples. *Solitude* naturally leads to *Community,* a
lifestyle with others who recognize and claim their
beloved nature as children of God. *Ministry* grows
from this community spirit, reaching out to a needy
world with the good news of God's love. Like Jesus,
if we spend intimate time with God, God's power
radiates to all with whom we come in contact.

*Solitude, community, and ministry create space for God to
work. Is your life lived in this order?*
Are times alone with God too few and far between?
*Are you trying to live life alone without the love and
support of community?*

*Has your life become self-focused, too isolated from ministry
and from the needs of others?*
*What needs to change for your life to become
more balanced and fruitful?*

Leave me alone with God as much as may be.
As the tide draws the waters close in upon the shore,
Make me an island, set apart,
alone with you, God, holy to you.
Then with the turning of the tide
prepare me to carry your presence to the busy world beyond,
the world that rushes in on me
till the waters come again and fold me back to you.

-Prayer of St. Aidan of Lindisfarne

BOAT

Throughout scripture, Jesus demonstrates his power over disease, demons, and death. He also reveals his power over nature after a long day of teaching along the Sea of Galilee. Jesus leads the disciples into a boat and when they push off from the shore they are met with nature's fury:

A GREAT WINDSTORM AROSE, AND THE WAVES BEAT INTO THE BOAT, SO THAT THE BOAT WAS ALREADY BEING SWAMPED. BUT [JESUS] WAS IN THE STERN, ASLEEP ON THE CUSHION; AND THEY WOKE HIM UP AND SAID TO HIM, "TEACHER, DO YOU NOT CARE THAT WE ARE PERISHING?" HE WOKE UP AND REBUKED THE WIND, AND SAID TO THE SEA, "PEACE! BE STILL!" THEN THE WIND CEASED, AND THERE WAS A DEAD CALM. HE SAID TO THEM, "WHY ARE YOU AFRAID? HAVE YOU STILL NO FAITH?" AND THEY WERE FILLED WITH GREAT AWE AND SAID TO ONE ANOTHER, "WHO THEN IS THIS, THAT EVEN THE WIND AND THE SEA OBEY HIM?

MARK 4:37-41 NRSV

When we experience a natural disaster, bankruptcy, layoff, the death of a loved one, or any number of unexpected catastrophes, we ask, "God, don't you care?" Just imagine these wet and cold, bruised and exhausted disciples, having fought the wind and waves for hours, finally crying out to Jesus, "Don't you care that we are perishing?" He responds with compassion. Sometimes Jesus calms the storm; at other times he calms the fear and storm within us.

In this story, what speaks to you the most? Is it that Jesus has power and authority over nature?

Or that the disciples ask Jesus for help, and then are shocked when he is able?

Or that Jesus is disappointed by their fear and doubt?

What does this story say about the mystery of God's presence in impossible situations?

Dear God
Be good to me
The sea is so wide and my boat is so small.

-Breton Sailor's Prayer

Ships were an early symbol of the Church,
an image of shelter from the storms of life—much like
Noah's Ark provided protection and salvation from the
great flood. Ships were also chosen because of the
association of Peter's fishing boat. The main part of a
church's interior, where the people worship, is called
a "nave," from the Latin "navis," or ship.

BROKEN SEASHELLS

A companion returned from her sunrise walk with a pocket full of broken shells. Responding to my doubtful look, she grinned and said, "They're broken—just like me. And look how beautiful they are!" As I examined them more closely, they were indeed beautiful in their intricate patterns, their brokenness revealing inner beauty often hidden in more perfect shells.

There is freedom in accepting our own brokenness. It takes a lot of energy to look and act perfect, to present an unblemished facade—in our attitudes, marriage, career, and our walk with God.

Please be patient—God isn't finished with me yet! When I am open and vulnerable about my brokenness, others feel accepted and safe to reveal their own wounds and faults. Together we discover the inner beauty in our unfinished souls still growing, seeking, learning ... a rich revelation left unseen when we don the mask of perfection.

Are you trying to present a mask of perfection?
How is God inviting you to recognize and accept your own brokenness?

God sees you with eyes full of love and mercy.
How can you see yourself in the same way, just as you are?

WE HAVE THIS TREASURE IN CLAY JARS,
SO THAT IT MAY BE MADE CLEAR THAT
THIS EXTRAORDINARY POWER BELONGS
TO GOD AND DOES NOT COME FROM US.
II COR. 4:7 NRSV

The world gives itself up to incessant activity merely because it knows of nothing better. The inspired man works among its whirring wheels also; but he knows whither the wheels are going, for he has found the centre where all is stillness …

-Paul Brunton

CENTERED

Imagine your life as a large wheel with many spokes. Too often we spend enormous amounts of time and energy running around the rim attempting to connect with everyone. But God's way is to stay in the middle hub, to live from the still center. In God's way, we stay connected with all the spokes without having to run so fast!

Draw a wheel in the sand, imagining that each spoke represents a facet of your life.
How is God inviting you to live in the still center hub?

In these days of intense distraction, I find it difficult to give my attention to any one thing. Multitasking, doing several things at once, without paying attention to any one thing, seems to be the norm. However, when I am unable or unwilling to stop and give my attention to a single task, all the tasks suffer. A phone conversation with a friend is diminished when I am also checking my email. A work task is done halfway when I attempt several chores at the same time.

And my connection with God suffers if I'm meditating as I rush out the door on my way to work. What I value deserves my full attention. God's love nourishes our attentiveness. When we are surrounded by distractions, fear or grief, God's love pierces our fogs and brings us closer to peace.

-Beth A. Richardson

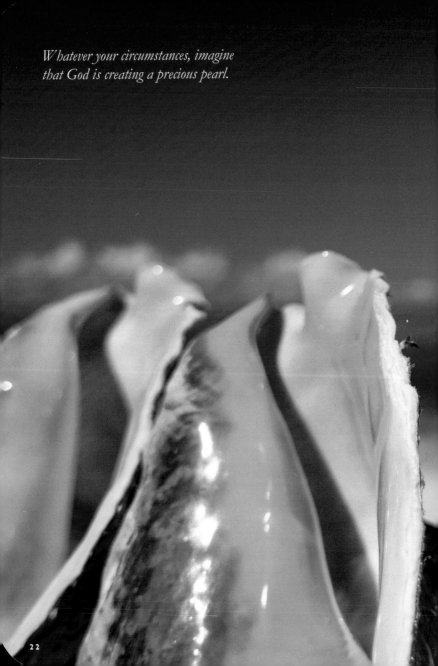

*Whatever your circumstances, imagine
that God is creating a precious pearl.*

CONCH SHELL

Its open mouth corresponds
to your own hunger to hear.
Rough as the bleat
of gulls, its edges
rasp your cheek, cold as salt;
the surge of sound floods
into your own convoluted
shell of an ear
through tympanum, stapes,
cochlea.
You lean into the roar—a tide
of air and water trapped
at the shell's pink, helical heart—
an ocean tumbled over
and over. Breath still moves
on the face of the deep;
you ached to its
tempest at your cheekbone.
And the inside tremor—
the thunder,
the wave that breaks over
more than your bare feet.
Listen deep until it owns you.
Know the whole world
a shell, and you the grit
caught in it, being pearled over.
-Luci Shaw

Besides hearing the word of God
through Scripture, through creation and
through one another, we can experience
the mystery of God deep within us at
the heart of our being. "Listen deep
until it owns you …" What cries do
you hear deep within you?

CONSERVATION

The Sea Around Us, written by ecologist Rachel Carson, offers a poignant lament of human impact on the oceans: "Man has written one of his blackest records as a destroyer on the oceanic islands. He has seldom set foot on an island that he has not brought about disastrous changes …

The tragedy of the oceanic islands lies in the uniqueness, the irreplaceability of the species they have developed over the slow processes of the ages. In a reasonable world men would have treated these islands as precious possessions, as natural museums filled with beautiful and curious works of creation, valuable beyond price because nowhere in the world are they duplicated."

From space, Earth has been described as a "blue marble" because 71% of the Earth's surface is ocean. All would agree that healthy oceans are vital to a healthy planet, useful for transportation, fishing, and exploration. But the health of our oceans is at risk. Air pollution is responsible for many of the toxic contaminants that end up in oceans and coastal waters from runoff via rivers and streams. Oil is one of the ocean's greatest resources, but is also one of the leading sources of pollution. Each year, three times as much garbage is dumped into the world's oceans as the weight of fish caught.

Do you take clean water, air,
and earth for granted?
The next time you turn on a water faucet,
thank God for sustaining the earth, sea, and sky.
Before God, will you pledge your "sustaining
love for creation"?

CREATION

Using the same old materials of earth, air, fire, and water, every twenty-four hours God creates something new out of them. If you think you're seeing the same show all over again seven times a week, you're crazy. Every morning you wake up to something that in all eternity never was before and never will be again. And the you that wakes up was never the same before and will never be the same again either.

-Frederick Buechner

The psalms teach us to lend our voice to all creatures: to the mountains and the waters; to the trees and the birds; to the light that comes from above and to the earth that provides for us; to the creatures of the sea, from the tiniest fish to the whale …

Ah, but would you like to have seen the splendor of the act of creation? Then just think, creation is made anew, instant by instant, at God's hands.

-Helder Camara

How do you greet a new day?
Same old, same old … or "something that
in all eternity never was before?"

Greet this day expectantly.
Pay attention and participate moment by
moment in the wonders of God's creation.

SING TO THE LORD A NEW SONG;
sing to the LORD, ALL THE EARTH ...
LET THE HEAVENS BE GLAD, AND LET
THE EARTH REJOICE; LET THE SEA ROAR,
AND ALL THAT FILLS IT.

PSALM 96:1, 11 NRSV

CREATIVITY

The world is full of creatures that for some reason seem stranger to us than others … hagfish, platypuses … butterflies emerging from anthills, spiderlings wafting through the air clutching tiny silken balloons, horseshoe crabs … The creator goes off on one wild, specific tangent after another, or millions simultaneously, with an exuberance that would seem to be unwarranted, and with an abandoned energy sprung from an unfathomable font. What is going on here? The point of the dragonfly's terrible lip, the giant water bug, birdsong, or the beautiful dazzle and flash of sunlighted minnows, is not that it all fits together like clockwork— for it doesn't, particularly, not even inside the goldfish bowl—but that it all flows so freely wild, like the creek, that it all surges in such a free, fringed tangle. Freedom is the world's water and weather, the world's nourishment freely given, its soil and sap: and the creator loves pizzazz.

-Annie Dillard

Since you are "made in the image of God," creativity is part of God's image that you bear.

Set yourself free to explore "one wild, specific tangent after another."
Be amazed at the beauty of God's lavish creativity.

How is God challenging you to
dream big, to sail out beyond
the safety of the shore, to live
boldly for God?

Pray that God keeps you on the
better way and never lets
you wander from God's purpose.

DARING

Disturb us, Lord, when
We are too well pleased with ourselves,
When our dreams have come true
Because we have dreamed too little,
When we arrived safely
Because we sailed too close to the shore.
Disturb us, Lord, when
With the abundance of things we possess
We have lost our thirst
For the waters of life;
Having fallen in love with life,
We have ceased to dream of eternity
And in our efforts to build a new earth,
We have allowed our vision
Of the new Heaven to dim.
Disturb us, Lord, to dare more boldly,
To venture on wider seas
Where storms will show your mastery;
Where losing sight of land,
We shall find the stars.
We ask You to push back
The horizons of our hopes;
And to push into the future
In strength, courage, hope, and love.

-Sir Francis Drake

Sir Francis Drake, the first English sea captain to circumnavigate the world, penned these words as he departed in 1577. Nothing is more dangerous than comfort and ease, subtly wooing us to accept whatever mediocre existence lies before us.

Left to ourselves, we are tempted to settle for the least, not the best. Like a river run wild, we take the path of least resistance, and assume it was the best route all along. How easily we set our lives on cruise control and move along merrily unaware that we are in fact drifting farther and farther away from God. Disturb us, Lord!

DAWN

Jesus walked through whispering wood:
'I am pale blossom, I am blood berry,
I am rough bark, I am sharp thorn.
This is the place where you will be born.'

Jesus went down to the skirl of the sea:
'I am long reach, I am fierce comber,
I am keen saltspray, I am spring tide.'
He pushed the cup of the sea aside.

And heard the sky which breathed-and-blew:
'I am the firmament, I am shape-changer,
I cradle and carry and kiss and roar,
I am infinite roof and floor.'

All day he walked, he walked all night,
Then Jesus came to the heart at dawn.
'Here and now,' said the heart-in-waiting,
'This is the place where you must be born.'

-Kevin Crossley-Holland

Jesus says that he is in all things,
from saltspray to the firmament.

How do you experience God on this seashore?
What is God birthing in you this new day?

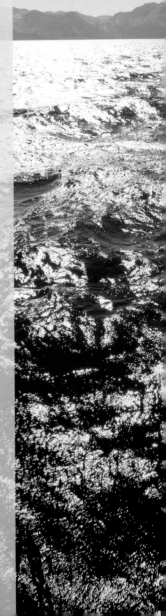

DEEP WATER

Jesus instructed his fishermen-disciples to cast their nets into the deep waters of the Sea of Galilee. They responded obediently and caught more fish than their boats could hold. In life, we are also invited into the deep to receive God's abundant blessings. We cannot fully grasp all that God has for us if we fear leaving the safety of the shore. If we only get our toes wet in shallow water, we will never know what blessings we have missed. Our needs can only be met when we "put out into the deep" and become completely submerged, bathed in life-giving water, soaked in the goodness of God.

"Deep calls to deep ..." (Ps. 42:7) Like the psalmist, the deepest part of me was created to be in communion with the deepness of God. The depth of who I am longs for this communion and will not be satisfied with anything less. This is a tender, interior space, beyond the reach of our rational minds, where the God who searches our hearts hears "our sighs too deep for words." (Romans 8:26)

LORD, take me deeper into You. Make me so comfortable in the sea of your love that I will more readily join You in the depths and not just wade in the shallows of your vast and immeasurable love. Amen.

-Leoma Gilley

Do you long for such deep intimacy with God?
What has you tied to shore,
* afraid to move into deep waters?*
Do you have courage and desire to enter the
* fathomless depths,*
* to be "all in"?*

*You, O eternal Trinity, are a deep sea into which, the
more I enter, and the more I find, the more I seek …*
   O abyss,
      O eternal Godhead,
         O sea profound,
what more could You give me than Yourself?

Catherine of Siena

DESPAIR

"IN TROUBLE, DEEP TROUBLE, I PRAYED TO GOD.
　　HE ANSWERED ME [JONAH.]
FROM THE BELLY OF THE GRAVE I CRIED, 'HELP!'
　　YOU HEARD MY CRY.
YOU THREW ME INTO OCEAN'S DEPTHS,
INTO A WATERY GRAVE,
WITH OCEAN WAVES, OCEAN BREAKERS
CRASHING OVER ME.
I SAID, 'I'VE BEEN THROWN AWAY,
　　THROWN OUT, OUT OF YOUR SIGHT' …
MY HEAD WAS ALL TANGLED IN SEAWEED
　　AT THE BOTTOM OF THE SEA WHERE THE
MOUNTAINS TAKE ROOT.
I WAS AS FAR DOWN AS A BODY CAN GO …
YET YOU PULLED ME UP FROM THAT GRAVE ALIVE,
　　O GOD, MY GOD!
WHEN MY LIFE WAS SLIPPING AWAY,
　　I REMEMBERED GOD,
AND MY PRAYER GOT THROUGH TO YOU …
I'M WORSHIPING YOU, GOD,
　　CALLING OUT IN THANKSGIVING!
AND I'LL DO WHAT I PROMISED I'D DO!
　　SALVATION BELONGS TO GOD!"
THEN GOD SPOKE TO THE FISH,
AND IT VOMITED UP JONAH ON THE SEASHORE.

-JONAH 2:1-10 THE MESSAGE

Realizing that he deserves death, Jonah offers this thanksgiving prayer for God's merciful deliverance after being swallowed by a whale. Although rarely as dramatic, most of us have experienced times of deep trouble when we also cried out, "I've been thrown away … out of your sight … as far down as a body can go." It may be a diagnosis, death, divorce, addiction, betrayal—whatever the cause, we feel abandoned and ready to give up. Yet it is in the deepest darkness that light shines brightest. In the depths of despair, we find hope.

As you gaze at the powerful ocean waves, remember a time when God rescued you "from the grave" and give thanks. If you are in a desperate season now, take hope that God hears your cries for help and will not let the waves of despair overwhelm you.

Come Thou Fount of every blessing
Tune my heart to sing Thy grace;
Streams of mercy, never ceasing,
Call for songs of loudest praise
Teach me some melodious sonnet,
Sung by flaming tongues above.
Praise the mount! I'm fixed upon it,
Mount of God's unchanging love.

O to grace how great a debtor
Daily I'm constrained to be!
Let that grace now like a fetter,
Bind my wandering heart to Thee.
Prone to wander, Lord, I feel it,
Prone to leave the God I love;
Here's my heart, O take and seal it,
Seal it for Thy courts above.

-Robert Robinson

DRIFTWOOD

Trees swept away by the sea become driftwood. When pieces of those trees return to shore smooth and sculpted, they can be used for furniture or decoration.
Like driftwood that never returns to shore, some of us drift away from faith. Sometimes we feel God has abandoned us or let us down and we're angry or hurt. At other times, people of God have let us down through neglect, judgment, or unkindness. Even when life is good and running smoothly, we can become distracted by a new relationship, a new home, or a new job and decide that we "don't need God right now."
To return to God's loving embrace, renewed and purified, we need to pray and express gratitude for our blessings.

SEARCH ME, O GOD, AND KNOW MY HEART; TEST ME AND KNOW MY THOUGHTS.
SEE IF THERE IS ANY WICKED WAY IN ME, AND LEAD ME IN THE WAY EVERLASTING.

PSALM 139:23-24 NRSV

Ask God to search your heart, revealing anything that may cause you to wander from God's grace.
Trust that even if you return broken and beat up, God sees you as whole and beautiful in spite of your scars.

DROP IN
THE OCEAN

Jesus died at 33, leaving Israel under the cruel domination of Roman rule. People still needed healing and others remained in desperate poverty. Yet at the end of his short life on Earth, Jesus said to God, his Father,

"I GLORIFIED YOU ON EARTH BY FINISHING THE WORK THAT YOU GAVE ME TO DO." JOHN 17:4 NRSV

I am often overwhelmed by the serious needs of people around me and can easily become discouraged that I am not doing enough to alleviate suffering. I realize that every need does not constitute a call, but discerning my unique calling can be difficult. I also realize that whatever I accomplish will seem small and insignificant. Yet however trivial, if I cheerfully offer my limited talents and resources, God will magnify them for Kingdom work in ways I may never know or understand. Instead of asking, "What difference can one person make?" I recall a childhood verse, echoing simple words of hope:

little drops of water
tiny grains of sand
make the mighty ocean
and the pleasant land

How might you, like Jesus, be confident in knowing what work you have to do?

How can you be faithful to your calling and generously offer what you have without feeling guilty about needs you haven't met?

We ourselves feel that what we are doing is just a drop in the ocean. But the ocean would be less because of that missing drop.

-Mother Teresa

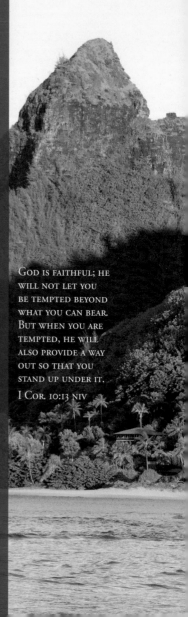

ESCAPE

After the Israelites escaped Egypt, they camped on the banks of the Red Sea. Looking up, they saw Pharaoh's entire army approaching from behind them. They were "terrified and cried out to the Lord ... Moses answered the people, 'Do not be afraid. Stand firm and you will see the deliverance the Lord will bring you today ... The Lord will fight for you; you need only to be still'." Then Moses raised his staff and the Sea parted and provided a way for the confused and frightened people to escape.

Ex. 14:10, 13-14 NIV

God does not part the Red Sea until we wade into the water. Only when we are in the midst of our trials and temptations does God provide a way of escape. When we are immersed so deeply that we cannot return but have no power to move forward, then God parts the sea and provides a way out of danger. In faith we cling to God's promises for deliverance, not because we understand what God is doing at the time, but because we trust that God is faithful and will fight for us.

Is your limited faith holding you back?
Are you waiting for God's "rescue"
from the safety of shore?
Claim God's promise to "fight for you"
and "be still."

God is faithful; he will not let you be tempted beyond what you can bear. But when you are tempted, he will also provide a way out so that you stand up under it.

I Cor. 10:13 NIV

ETERNITY

He moves mountains
without their knowing it
and overturns them in his
anger.
He shakes the earth from its
place and makes its pillars tremble.
He speaks to the sun and it does
not shine; he seals off the light of
the stars.
He alone stretches out the
heavens and treads on the waves of
the sea.
He is the Maker of the Bear and
Orion, the Pleiades and the
constellations of the south.
He performs wonders that
cannot be fathomed, miracles
that cannot be counted.

Job 9:5-10 NIV

Standing before the Creator, we realize
once again that we are not the center of
the universe.

Humbled like Job, we become
content to be the created being and not
the omnipotent Creator.

Ask God to open your eyes to the
mysteries of creation, as God opened
Job's so long ago.

The oceans connect us with our past, present, and future. The waves that we enjoy today at Daytona Beach or LaJolla may have been frozen in an Arctic glacier or shimmered in the Mediterranean years ago before they journeyed through unseen currents to these shores.

Marine biologist Rachel Carson observes in *The Sea Around Us*, "In its mysterious past [the sea] encompasses all the dim origins of life and receives in the end, after, it may be, many transmutations, the dead husks of that same life. For all at last return to the sea—to Oceanus, the ocean river, like the ever-flowing stream of time, the beginning and the end."

In *Under the Sea Wind*, Carson marvels, "To stand at the edge of the sea, to sense the ebb and the flow of the tides, to feel the breath of a mist moving over a great salt marsh, to watch the flight of shore birds that have swept up and down the surf lines of the continents for untold thousands of years, to see the running of the old eels and the young shad to the sea, is to have knowledge of things that are as nearly eternal as any earthly life can be."

FISH

The simple fish was one of the most familiar symbols of Christ in the early Church and can be found in early places of worship, as well as the catacombs. In Greek, the phrase, "Jesus Christ, Son of God Savior," is *"Iesous Christos Theou Yios Soter."* The first letters of each of these Greek words, when put together, spell *"ichthys,"* the Greek word for "fish" (ΙΧΘΥΣ).

The earliest literary reference to the fish as a Christian symbol was made by Clement of Alexandria, who advised Christians to use a dove or fish as their seal. Tertullian wrote, "But we, being little fishes, as Jesus Christ is our great Fish, begin our life in the water, and only while we abide in the water are we safe and sound."

The *ichthys* fish is also a symbol for the story of Jesus' miracle feeding over five thousand people with a few loaves of bread and a few fish. This photo shows a tile mosaic created around 480 AD on the floor of the Church of the Multiplication, a Tabgha church on the Sea of Galilee.

I GIVE YOU A NEW
COMMANDMENT THAT YOU
LOVE ONE ANOTHER. JUST
AS I HAVE LOVED YOU, YOU
ALSO SHOULD LOVE ONE
ANOTHER. BY THIS
EVERYONE WILL KNOW THAT
YOU ARE MY DISCIPLES,
IF YOU HAVE LOVE FOR ONE
ANOTHER.

JOHN 13:34-35 NRSV

Modern Christians sometimes
display early Christian symbols
in personal art, jewelry, or even
bumper stickers.

If you are identified as a
Christian by those around you,
does your example reveal the
fruit of God's Spirit?

FISHERMEN

As [Jesus] walked by the Sea of Galilee, he saw two brothers, Simon, who is called Peter, and Andrew his brother, casting a net into the sea—for they were fishermen. And he said to them, "Follow me, and I will make you fish for people."

Matthew 4:19 NRSV

We want to leave our mark, to let people know we were here on this earth. We carve on trees, write graffiti on walls, build pyramids and monuments. We seek ways to say someone was here and did something worth remembering.

God leaves his mark everywhere—on all creation, every nation, every face. God's signature is all around. If we learn to live like God, we also can leave a lasting mark behind. When we invest our time, resources, and love into the people surrounding us, we can be assured that God is using us to transform them into God's image. This leaves an everlasting mark, whether we see immediate results or not. Hear God's promise:

Because you are precious in my sight, and honored, and I love you, I give people in return for you, nations in exchange for your life.

Is. 43:4 NRSV

Do you believe that God can and will use you in the lives of others?
Do you pray for and serve others as often as you worry about investing in worldly assets and finances?
Are you investing your life into relationships and things of eternal value?

FLOATING

As swimmers dare
to lie face to the sky
and water bears them,
as hawks rest upon air
and air sustains them,
so would I learn to attain
freefall, and float
into Creator Spirit's deep embrace,
knowing no effort earns
that all-surrounding grace.

-Denise Levertov, The Avowal

Into your arms, loving Lord,
    let me "freefall,"
        upheld by your goodness
            and mercy.
Secure in your embrace,
    show me how to
        love without effort,
            trust without fear,
            and live with abandon.

-Sam Hamilton-Poore

*Float freely on the waves, aware of any
tension in your body.
You can only float when you rest and
trust the saltwater to hold you.*

*What is dragging you down in life?
What do you need to let go?
How is God inviting you to trust
more completely?*

FOOTPRINTS IN THE SAND

One night I dreamed I was walking along the beach with the Lord. Many scenes from my life flashed across the sky. In each scene I noticed footprints in the sand. Sometimes there were two sets of footprints, other times there was one only.

This bothered me because I noticed that during the low periods of my life, when I was suffering from anguish, sorrow or defeat, I could see only one set of footprints, so I said to the Lord, "You promised me Lord, that if I followed you, you would walk with me always. But I have noticed that during the most trying periods of my life there has only been one set of footprints in the sand. Why, when I needed you most, have you not been there for me?"

The Lord replied, "The years when you have seen only one set of footprints, my child, is when I carried you."

-Mary Stevenson

God doesn't promise the absence of trouble, but promises to be present with us. God didn't come to take our suffering away, but to become part of it. Ponder the "low" periods in your life, times of sorrow and defeat.

How did you experience God carrying you when you suffered most?

EVEN TO YOUR OLD AGE AND GRAY HAIRS
I AM HE, I AM HE WHO WILL SUSTAIN YOU.
I HAVE MADE YOU AND I WILL CARRY YOU;
I WILL SUSTAIN YOU AND I WILL RESCUE YOU.

ISAIAH 46:4 NIV

Who is a God like you, who pardons sin and forgives … ? You will again have compassion on us; you will tread our sins underfoot and hurl our iniquities into the depths of the sea.

Micah 7:18-19 niv

© iStock/Christine Ge

FORGIVENESS

Corrie Ten Boom was imprisoned in a German concentration camp for sheltering Jews in Holland. After her release, Corrie struggled to forgive those who had abused her and killed her entire family. She spent the rest of her life traveling the world to share her simple Gospel message of God's love and forgiveness.

In one talk, wanting to emphasize that God's forgiveness is permanent, she shared a simple, but profound, example. She said that when we confess our sins, God casts them into the depths of the sea and puts up a sign: NO FISHING ALLOWED!

Are there sins that linger in your mind, seemingly impossible to forgive or forget?
Are you struggling to forgive someone who has sinned against you?
If God has forgiven you—and them—why are you still clinging to guilt and resentment?

Choose a rock or shell and let it represent your offenses against God.
After confession, hurl all your hurts and hidden faults into the depths of the sea and resolve to leave them there!
Express your gratitude for God's undeserved forgiveness and grace.

FREEDOM

I must go down to the seas again, to the lonely sea and the sky,
And all I ask is a tall ship and a star to steer her by,
And the wheel's kick and the wind's song and the white sail's shaking,
And a grey mist on the sea's face, and a grey dawn breaking,

I must go down to the seas again, for the call of the running tide
Is a wild call and a clear call that may not be denied;
And all I ask is a windy day with the white clouds flying,
And the flung spray and the blown spume, and the sea-gulls crying.

I must go down to the seas again, to the vagrant gypsy life,
To the gull's way and the whale's way where the wind's like a whetted knife;
And all I ask is a merry yarn from a laughing fellow-rover,
And quiet sleep and a sweet dream when the long trick's over.

-John Masefield, Sea Fever

A former sailor, the author remembers the loneliness and quiet of the open sea. He longs for a well-built ship, strong winds to sail, and a guiding star in the night sky. The old sailor laments his former life on the seas and is nostalgic for monadic life, that of a wanderer with no permanent home.

He still feels the wind and salt spray on his face, sees the stars and the grey mist of dawn, hears the wild cry of the gulls and his old friends telling their tall tales, and recalls being lulled into gentle sleep. The call to return to adventure on the high seas cannot be ignored and he resolutely vows to return.

What memories will you take from this pilgrim walk at the sea?

Using all your senses, describe in your journal what you will remember.

The only active sailing vessel in the U.S. naval services, the Eagle is anchored at the Coast Guard Academy in New London, Connecticut. Saluting the Eagle and all Tall Ships (sailing vessels) in 1986, Ronald Reagan said: "These vessels embody our conception of liberty itself; to have no impediments, only open spaces to chart one's own course, to take adventure as it comes, to be as free as the wind, as free as the tall ships themselves."

© Tandem/Matthew Kuhns

FUTILITY

Vanity of vanities, says the Teacher, vanity
of vanities! All is vanity.
What do people gain from all the toil at
which they toil under the sun?
A generation goes, and a generation comes,
but the earth remains forever.
The sun rises and the sun goes down, and
hurries to the place where it rises ...
All streams run to the sea, but the sea is
not full;
  to the place where the streams flow,
there they continue to flow.
All things are wearisome; more than one
can express;
  the eye is not satisfied with seeing, or
the ear filled with hearing.
What has been is what will be, and what
has been done is what will be done;
  there is nothing new under the sun ...
All is vanity and a chasing after wind.

Eccles. 1: 2-9, 14 nrsv

Reflecting on his long life, an old man sees humans
in mad pursuit of one thing and then another—
laboring as if they could master the universe, vainly
pursuing success that in reality is meaningless and
"a chasing after wind." Life without God has no
purpose and no satisfaction. Faith teaches the
author of Ecclesiastes that God controls all things
for God's purposes and that the role of humans is
to accept their limitations and to gratefully enjoy
God's gift of abundant life.

Does your striving often
seem meaningless?
To find your purpose, are there areas of your
life that need to be surrendered to God?

Consider the mystery that "all streams run to
the sea, but the sea is not full."
Ponder how Creator God has established all
nature to function in harmony.

GEESE

The wild goose is an ancient Celtic symbol of the Holy Spirit. Although familiar with the traditional symbol of gentle doves, Celtic Christians chose the wild goose as a reminder that the Spirit of God cannot be tamed or controlled.

Wild geese have a habit of biting those who try to contain or capture them. Each time the religious establishment appeared to be firmly in control of theology and God, the Spirit of God broke free—and often bit those who tried to stop it. Whenever the church settled into complacent institutional apathy, Spirit-filled people boldly advocated for the gospel's radical demands.

Wild geese also have a habit of making a lot of noise when you disturb them. The song of the goose is considered harsh and noisy, not unlike the voices of reformers who clamored for renewal, truth, and justice. Over the centuries, those in power ostracized, imprisoned, exiled, and even killed wild goose Christians. But the noisy, passionate courage of these Spirit-led men and women helped recapture the original Christian vision that the gospel cannot be curbed or restricted.

The wild goose is a communal creature, drawing its life from the flock. In the same way, God's Spirit is not a spirit of individualism, but of community. In an age when an independent spirit is prevalent both inside and outside the church, we remember the earliest Christians testifying that the Spirit brings people together into community.

How do you experience God's Spirit? Have you found yourself advocating for reform when the Church becomes complacent?

Have you judged and tried to silence those who work for transformation, threatening the prevailing "peace and unity of the church"?

AFTER [PETER AND JOHN] PRAYED, THE PLACE WHERE THEY
WERE MEETING WAS SHAKEN. AND THEY WERE ALL FILLED WITH
THE HOLY SPIRIT AND SPOKE THE WORD OF GOD BOLDLY.
ACTS 4:31 NIV

GENEROSITY

When I was a child,
I gave him all I had.
He stood among hungry people
who needed fed.
And I believed that he knew
how to make the food go round.
Now that I am an adult,
I have much more to share.
But, though the crowds are still hungry,
I am reluctant to give him what I have.
Lord, when today I see the face of those
who long for food and justice,
when I hear their cry,
make me as generous as when I was a child.

-John L. Bell

All four Gospels tell the story of Jesus
instructing his disciples to feed a hungry crowd
at the end of a long day. Taking stock of their
remote hillside, the disciples could only find
a young boy willing to share five barley loaves
and two small fish and they questioned how far
the provisions would go among so many. But
Jesus thanked God for what they had and then
watched the meager provisions multiply enough
to feed over five thousand people.

Are you reluctant to give away your possessions?
Overwhelmed with the serious needs of the world,
do you wish you had more to give?

Take inventory of your own resources, whether
bountiful or meager: all your personal, material, family,
intellectual, physical, and spiritual resources.
Imagine yourself putting everything into Jesus'
hands to use and multiply for good.

GOD'S LOVE WAS REVEALED AMONG US IN THIS WAY: GOD SENT
HIS ONLY SON INTO THE WORLD SO THAT WE MIGHT LIVE
THROUGH HIM ... SINCE GOD LOVED US SO MUCH, WE ALSO
OUGHT TO LOVE ONE ANOTHER.

I JOHN 4:9, 11 NRSV

GOD'S LOVE

This verse from an old hymn expresses the impossibility of ever adequately expressing God's unfathomable, unconditional love:

Could we with ink the ocean fill,
And were the skies of parchment made,
Were every stalk on earth a quill,
And every man a scribe by trade,
To write the love of God above,
Would drain the ocean dry.
Nor could the scroll contain the whole,
Though stretched from sky to sky.

O love of God, how rich and pure!
How measureless and strong!
It shall forevermore endure
The saints' and angels' song.

-Martin Lehman

Realize that there is nothing you can do to make God love you any more and there is nothing you can do that would make God love you any less.

Say or write a simple prayer thanking God for such "measureless and strong" love.

GRATITUDE

Some went down to the sea in ships,
    doing business on the mighty waters;
    they saw the deeds of the LORD,
his wondrous works in the deep.
For he commanded and raised the stormy wind,
which lifted up the waves of the sea.
They mounted up to heaven, they went down to the depths;
their courage melted away in their calamity;
they reeled and staggered like drunkards,
and were at their wits' end.
Then they cried to the LORD in their trouble,
and he brought them out from their distress;
he made the storm be still,
and the waves of the sea were hushed.
Then they were glad because they had quiet,
and he brought them to their desired haven.
Let them thank the LORD for his steadfast love,
for his wonderful works to humankind.

PSALM 107:23-31 NRSV

Psalm 107 begins: "O give thanks to the Lord, for he is good;
for his steadfast love endures forever" and continues with
four perilous situations when people cried out to God for
deliverance. God is a magnet for our cries of helplessness
when we admit our absolute need. While the modern phrase
says that "God helps those who help themselves," God helps
those who are helpless.

At the conclusion of each desperate situation, the people gave
thanks. The Hebrew word for "thanks" is "todah," meaning
to give a tangible thank offering, an identifiable expression
of huge gratitude for what God does that we could never do
ourselves.

Reflect on ways God has rescued you from danger—
an accident, natural disaster, disease, etc.
Have you thanked God for deliverance?
What could you give as a "thank offering,"
a tangible reminder of your gratitude?

GREY SEAS

The soul remembered how when she was a very little girl she had sympathized with the grey sea. The blue sea was a happy sea. The green sea, when the waves thereof tossed themselves and roared, was a triumphant sea. But the grey sea looked anxious. So the child was sorry for the grey sea. Grey weather she abhorred. Something of this feeling was with her still. Grey weather was not among the things for which she gave thanks. Then God her Father said to her: All weathers nourish souls.

-Amy Carmichael

Most of us prefer the bright blue skies of summer to the dreary grey of winter, but we realize that both are necessary weather patterns. We humans also experience varied seasons. Some are filled with new life and promise, hope and fruitfulness, while others are depressing with their stagnant growth, grief, and times of limited or no apparent productiveness. Healthy souls choose to appreciate the value of change and the benefits which each season offers.

What season of life are you experiencing now?
If it is a time of new growth and promise, give thanks.
If it is a time of shattered dreams and darkness, give thanks.

Look for God's loving hand in every season, for "all
weathers nourish souls."

God is good … he who gives us our lives not only rules over us but loves us, likes us, is for us and not against us. Out of this realization comes the ability to receive the events of life with gratitude, not resentment, and to regard them as expressions of mysterious love … Instead of seeing [problems] as hopeless obstacles to our happiness, we come to see them as the challenges that give life its meaning and excitement.

-John Claypool

GIVE THANKS IN ALL CIRCUMSTANCES ... I Thess. 5:18 NIV

As a pilgrim tonight on this seashore is God leading you
to walk "by another [unfamiliar] route"?
Do you trust God to be your Guide,
leading you onward?
Ask God to use "cloud," "fire," and "stars"
to move you into places of service.

GUIDANCE

THE STAR THEY HAD SEEN IN THE EAST WENT AHEAD OF THEM UNTIL IT STOPPED OVER THE PLACE WHERE THE CHILD WAS. WHEN THEY SAW THE STAR, THEY WERE OVERJOYED. ON COMING TO THE HOUSE, THEY SAW THE CHILD WITH HIS MOTHER MARY, AND THEY BOWED DOWN AND WORSHIPED HIM ... AND HAVING BEEN WARNED IN A DREAM NOT TO GO BACK TO HEROD, THEY RETURNED TO THEIR COUNTRY BY ANOTHER ROUTE.

MATTHEW 2:9-12 NIV

The first pilgrims in Christ's story are the Magi in search of the promised child. Ultimately, pilgrimage invites us to follow a star, the reflection of God's spirit within us. Patient seeking will lead us to God, just as the Magi were guided by a star to Bethlehem and into the presence of the Christ Child.

Earlier in the biblical story, when the people of Israel wandered in the desert, God provided just what they needed by sending a pillar of fire by night when the desert was cold and a pillar of cloud by day when the desert sun was blazing hot:

BY DAY THE LORD WENT AHEAD OF THEM IN A PILLAR OF CLOUD TO GUIDE THEM ON THEIR WAY AND BY NIGHT IN A PILLAR OF FIRE TO GIVE THEM LIGHT, SO THAT THEY COULD TRAVEL BY DAY OR NIGHT. NEITHER THE PILLAR OF CLOUD BY DAY NOR THE PILLAR OF FIRE BY NIGHT LEFT ITS PLACE IN FRONT OF THE PEOPLE.

EXODUS 13:21-22 NIV

May the stars light your way and may you find the interior road.

-Irish farewell prayer

HARBOR

GOD IS OUR REFUGE AND STRENGTH, A VERY PRESENT HELP IN TROUBLE. Ps. 46:1 NRSV

A harbor is a body of water along the shore deep enough for anchoring ships and providing protection from winds, waves, and currents. Harbors usually have docks or ports and are considered places of refuge or shelter. Just as ships need safe havens to seek shelter, we, too, need safe havens from the storms in our lives.

In *Convivio*, Italian author, Dante Alighieri, describes death as our safe harbor after life's long voyage: "Just as a good mariner when he draws near to the harbor, lets down his sails, and enters it gently with slight headway on; so we ought to let down the sails of our worldly pursuits, and turn to God with all our understanding and heart, so that we may come to that haven with all composure and with all peace."

*Where and with whom
do you feel most safe?
How can you be a safe haven
for others on life's dangerous
journey?*

Do you not know that you are
God's temple and that God's
Spirit dwells in you? … God's
temple is holy, and you are
that temple.

I Cor. 3:16-17   nrsv

HERMIT CRAB

These unusual crabs live in borrowed empty shells and carry their houses with them wherever they go. They need protection because they have a soft body, so when they find an empty, clean shell that's the right size, they back into it, hooking themselves in with their back legs. Like lobsters, they have two large front claws that they use to seal off the opening of the shell for extra protection. The hermit crab lives in his borrowed shell until he outgrows it and must find a new, larger shell.

We also live in a borrowed house that goes wherever we go …

Consider what you eat and how well you rest and exercise.

How can you take better care of your body, the temporary house God has given you?

HERON

As I drive home on a narrow curving road, someone tailgates, itching to go faster, not knowing he's flesh and fragile. Slowed by sadness and sick of pressure, I pull onto the gravel shoulder, let him shoot by, and on my right catch sight of a great blue heron standing tall and still in the aisle made by two rows of towering trees. Like a priest in feathered robes, he bows his head three times before an altar of mountain bluffs. It's dusk, and the moon, just rising, illuminates his wings as they open in benediction for evening flight. His parting call: "Stay awake, Holiness may spread its wings for you at any moment."

-Patricia A. Lunetta

In what ways are you like the hurried tailgater?

How is God inviting you to stop, look, and listen to the wisdom found in nature?

Referring to God's sure promise of the Messiah, the apostle Paul says: "We have this hope as an anchor for the soul, firm and secure."

HEBREWS 6:19A NIV

HOPE

Early Christians adopted the dolphin as a common symbol of their faith, in addition to the generic fish icon. Dolphins are social creatures that create strong bonds and care for one another, even feeding and pushing a sick animal to the surface to breathe. Attracted by the dolphin's strength and swiftness, its beauty and affectionate disposition, ancients likened it to the divine nature in humankind, and the image was later adopted to represent Christ, the God-Man.

Anchors were a familiar symbol of hope and safety in the early Church. Thus the dolphin winding itself around an anchor was used to symbolize Christ on the cross and express hope and confidence in the Savior.

The composite symbol of strong dolphin and firm anchor was engraved upon household items, rings, and tombs of early Christians, signifying that the owner was a faithful follower of Christ.

Enjoy the antics of playful dolphins offshore. What might you choose as an appropriate symbol for your own faith?

ISLAND

No man is an island,
Entire of itself,
Every man is a piece
of the continent,
A part of the main.
If a clod be washed away by
the sea,
Europe is the less.
As well as if a promontory
were.
As well as if a manor of thy
friend's
Or of thine own were:
Any man's death diminishes
me,
Because I am involved in
mankind,
And therefore never send to
know for whom the bell tolls;
It tolls for thee.

-John Donne

Though each individual stands uniquely alone like an island, each of us is part of the whole. Even when we clamor for independence, we need healthy relationships to survive. People are interconnected; we are designed as social beings, never intended to live in isolation. There are no human islands.

Facing a life-threatening illness, Donne was keenly aware of his own mortality as he penned these words. The death of an individual—signified by the tolling of the bell—affects us all. Donne affirms that each death diminishes all of us, since we are all connected..

Is your life too isolated?
How can you foster healthier relationships?

JOURNEY

Sea-polished stones
did you welcome them
as they waded ashore,
guiding with calloused hand
coracles among the rocks?
And did the sucking sea
tug at their feet as
Erin tugged at their hearts?

With what dismay did they
remember the oaks of Derry,
warm hearths and friends?
Cold the cry of seagulls,
curious the bobbing seals,
bleak the mists of
moorland and machair.

Then through the gloom,
glowing as the day dawns,
a fire—and, dimly seen,
arms outstretched in greeting,
Columba stands. Beside him,
some fish, some bread, and
breaking upon their spirits the
reminder of another Man,
another place …

-Fiona Martin

*Although most of us will never
have to risk such a journey, there
are times when God calls us to
launch into unknown seas with
faith, trusting that Jesus will meet
us there.*

*In what way are you being invit-
ed to move toward an unknown
future, leaving your familiar
"warm hearth and friends"?*

*Can you trust God to be with
you, even if only "dimly seen"?*

As Irish monks continued to
make the perilous journey
across desolate seas to the
remote island of Iona,
Columba greeted them just as
Christ greeted the bewildered
disciples on the Galilean
shore:

WHEN [THE DISCIPLES] HAD
GONE ASHORE THEY SAW A
CHARCOAL FIRE THERE, WITH
FISH ON IT, AND BREAD. JESUS
SAID TO THEM … "COME
AND HAVE BREAKFAST"… THIS
WAS NOW THE THIRD TIME
THAT JESUS APPEARED TO THE
DISCIPLES AFTER HE WAS RAISED
FROM THE DEAD.

JOHN 21:9, 12, 14 NRSV

KELP

W E HAVE THIS HOPE [IN CHRIST], A SURE AND STEADFAST ANCHOR OF THE SOUL.

HEBREWS 6:19A NRSV

One of many algae found in the sea, kelp doesn't have roots to absorb nutrients and water as terrestrial plants do. Instead, it has a "holdfast" that anchors it to the bottom of the rocky sea floor while air-filled bladders allow the kelp to float and grow upward toward the light. Most holdfasts are small compared to the size of the kelp, but they are strong enough to maintain the kelp's position, even in turbulent waves and stormy seas. Kelp can grow up to 250 feet high—as tall as a 25-story building!

Once we are anchored in the Rock of Ages, we also grow toward God's Light. As long as we stay moored by faith, we can thrive no matter how overwhelming our trials. We only need to hold on tight and look up!

Is your faith "firm and secure"? Who or what do you trust to anchor you during life's storms?

In his lengthy poem, "The Lighthouse,"
Henry Wadsworth Longfellow recalls
growing up near such a steadfast
lighthouse beam:

… The mariner remembers when a child,
on his first voyage, he saw it fade and sink
And when returning from adventures wild,
He saw it rise again o'er ocean's brink.
Steadfast, serene, immovable, the same,
Year after year, through all the silent night
Burns on forevermore that quenchless flame,
Shines on that inextinguishable light!

Light a candle and marvel at how far its light penetrates the darkness. Where do you seek light and guidance when you're navigating troubled waters?

LIGHTHOUSE

Lighthouses were used along shorelines to guide and protect sailors, directing them away from dangerous rocks and sandbars and into safer waters. Modern technology has replaced lighthouse beacons that warned of danger when skies were too dark or stormy to see the coast, but many lighthouses remain as symbols of dedication, guidance, hope, and steadfastness. For many Christians, lighthouses represent Christ who is always with us, shining his light when we navigate difficult times. God's Word provides guidance, protection, comfort and hope for those who are lost.

"You have access to the lighthouse of the Lord. There is no fog so dense, no night so dark, no mariner so lost, no gale so strong as to render useless the lighthouse of the Lord. It beckons through the storms of life. It seems to call, 'This way to safety; this way to home.'"

-S. Monson

THE PEOPLE WHO WALKED IN DARKNESS HAVE SEEN A GREAT LIGHT, THOSE WHO LIVED IN A LAND OF DEEP DARKNESS—ON THEM LIGHT HAS SHINED.

ISAIAH 9:2 NRSV

THE LORD IS MY LIGHT AND MY SALVATION; WHOM SHALL I FEAR? THE LORD IS THE STRONG-HOLD OF MY LIFE; OF WHOM SHALL I BE AFRAID?

PS. 27:1 NRSV

MERCY

There's a wideness in God's mercy like the wideness of the sea; there's a kindness in God's justice, which is more than liberty.

For the love of God is broader than the measure of our mind; and the heart of the Eternal is most wonderfully kind.

If our love were but more simple, we should rest upon God's word; and our lives would be illumined by the presence of our Lord.

-Frederick W. Faber

Is God's mercy big enough to encompass all those who think and act differently from me?

Is God's mercy big enough, his justice kind enough, to accept even me? If so, what keeps me from extending the same liberty to others that I have received?

Who needs to experience God's mercy through you?

In essentials, unity;
in non-essentials, liberty;
in all things, charity.

-St. Augustine of Hippo

MOON

The *Carmina Gadelica* is a collection of sung prayers from a hardy sea-going people in the outer Hebrides off the northwest coast of Scotland. These homely people prayed their needs with simple intimacy, as well as awe and deference, sprinkling them with the vigor and humor that characterized their lives. There was no separation between sacred and mundane as all creation was esteemed in common: the Trinity of God, humankind, and all living creatures.

Esther de Waal explains, "At the heart of this sense of unity lies the recognition that everything good comes fromGod and is to be given freedom to be itself, to enjoy and be enjoyed, and that we are enslaved if we care for anything in ways that exclude the Giver."

Celtic Christians had no trouble recognizing that the world is God's and full of God's glory. Their simple prayers recited throughout the day reflect this understanding. Traditionally, they would pray the following on the night of the new moon:

He Who created thee
Created me likewise;
He who gave thee weight and light
Gave to me life and death.

-Carmina Gadelica

Say this little prayer when you see manifestations of God's creation—moon, stars, blue sky, clouds, birds and sea creatures.

As you gaze at creation, pray, "He Who created thee created me likewise." Be mindful of changes in your awareness.

MOON AND TIDES

Tides are the alternating rise and fall of sea levels caused by the gravitational pull of the moon and sun and the rotation of the Earth. As the moon travels around the Earth, and as the moon and earth together travel around the sun, the combined gravitational forces cause the world's ocean levels to rise and fall. Since the earth is rotating while this is happening, two tides fluctuate each day.

Imagine the mysterious and powerful forces of gravity that affect the tides, and the wind and ocean currents that affect the waves. We are usually unaware of this cosmic interaction, yet it continues uninterrupted day after day. Whether the moon shows full, as a tiny sliver, or is hidden by clouds, it continues to exert its pull on the waters of the earth.

In the same way, whether we are aware of the presence of God or not, God continues to sustain the Earth. Sometimes God feels close and at other times, distant or silent, but regardless of our perception, God is always present. Just as the tide comes in and draws out, ebbing and flowing each day, God's love pours out unceasingly in a divine tide, giving us mercy and grace and receiving our praise and gratitude.

AM I A GOD NEAR BY … AND NOT A GOD FAR OFF? WHO CAN HIDE IN SECRET PLACES SO THAT I CANNOT SEE THEM? … DO I NOT FILL HEAVEN AND EARTH? SAYS THE LORD.

JEREMIAH 23:23-24 NRSV

WHY IS IT EASIER TO BELIEVE THAT THE MOON REMAINS
IN THE SKY THOUGH IT IS HIDDEN, THAN TO BELIEVE THAT
GOD IS AT WORK WHEN GOD APPEARS DISTANT OR SILENT?
PRAY FOR FAITH TO BELIEVE,
"THE ASSURANCE OF THINGS HOPED FOR, THE
CONVICTION OF THINGS NOT SEEN."

HEBREWS 11:1 NRSV

NIGHT

Thanks be to you, O God,
for the night and its light,
for stars that emerge out of evening skies
and the white moon's radiance.
Thanks be to you
for the earth's unfolding of colour
and the bright sheen of creatures from ocean depths.
In the darknesses of the world
and in the night of my own soul
let me be looking with longing for light
let me be looking in hope.

-J. Philip Newell

Nobody is wise who does not know darkness.
I appreciate the dark hours of my existence
in which my senses are sharpened.

-Lucile H. Jones

St. Ignatius of Loyola encouraged a daily
"examination of consciousness" to recognize what
brings both life and death to our souls. Examen
brings to mind things we might otherwise miss in the
busyness of our lives. Ask two questions at the end
of the day:
1) When did I feel most loved and alive, closest to
others and God? What or who gave me energy and
joy? Offer thanks to God.
2) When did I feel unloved or distant from others
and God? What or who drained my energy and joy?
Confess any instance when you failed to be a faithful
disciple. Ask and receive God's forgiveness.

Practicing examen is one way to "search my spirit"
and to "[look] with longing for light."

What truths of God allow you to
be "looking in hope"?

I COMMUNE WITH
MY HEART IN THE
NIGHT, I MEDITATE
AND SEARCH MY
SPIRIT.

PS. 77:6 NRSV

ORIGINALITY

Form is certainty. All nature knows this, and we have no greater adviser. Clouds have forms, porous and shape-shifting, bumptious, fleecy. They are what clouds need to be, to be clouds. See a flock of them come, on the sled of the wind, all kneeling above the blue sea. And in the blue water, see the dolphin built to leap, the sea mouse skittering, see the ropy kelp with its air-filled bladders tugging it upward; see the albatross floating day after day on its three-jointed wings. Each form sets a tone, enables a destiny, strikes a note in the universe unlike any other. How can we ever stop looking? How can we ever turn away?

-Mary Oliver

A television show about amphibians featured a Japanese woman who had devoted her life to researching giant salamanders. Holding up a huge, brown, slimy blob with fierce teeth, she said with a shy smile, "I know many people find them ugly, but I find them beautiful. I love these creatures and I feel lucky that I get to study them."

Reflecting on the woman's comments, Christian author, Brian McLaren writes, "At that moment I thought: maybe God allows each of us to join God in loving some special aspect of creation, from weather to stars to dinosaurs to rocks to antique cars to songbirds to lions to electricity to wines to motorcycles to giant salamanders. If that's the case, I get the honor of joining the Creator in appreciating turtles. You might think my Japanese counterpart and I are strange, but we actually feel quite lucky."

How do you "join God in loving some special aspect of creation"?

© YASUMITIAN SU

HE TENDS HIS FLOCK LIKE A SHEPHERD:
HE GATHERS THE LAMBS IN HIS ARMS AND
CARRIES THEM CLOSE TO HIS HEART;
HE GENTLY LEADS THOSE THAT HAVE YOUNG.

ISAIAH 40:11 NIV

OSPREYS

Ospreys are one of the most common raptors. These birds of prey hunt for food in flight using their keen senses, and their vision is well adapted to detecting underwater objects from the air. After they spot prey, the birds hover momentarily before plunging feet first into the water.

In the morning when the sun is in the east, the mother osprey has her chicks move to the far side of the nest and she stands in front of them and holds her wings out part way to shield them from the sun. In the afternoon, she repeats the process, this time standing to the west of her chicks to block the sun's rays.

If only every parent was this attentive to the needs of their children! The apostle Paul demonstrated such love in describing his relationship with the church in Thessalonica:

"WE WERE GENTLE AMONG YOU, LIKE A MOTHER CARING FOR HER LITTLE CHILDREN. WE LOVED YOU SO MUCH THAT WE WERE DELIGHTED TO SHARE WITH YOU NOT ONLY THE GOSPEL OF GOD, BUT OUR LIVES AS WELL, BECAUSE YOU HAD BECOME SO DEAR TO US ... FOR YOU KNOW THAT WE DEALT WITH EACH OF YOU AS A FATHER DEALS WITH HIS OWN CHILDREN, ENCOURAGING, COMFORTING, AND URGING YOU TO LIVE LIVES WORTHY OF GOD, WHO CALLS YOU INTO HIS KINGDOM AND GLORY."

I THESS. 2:7-8, 11-12 NIV

What is your vision of God? Is God a demanding judge, standing ready to condemn ... or is God like a gentle shepherd, tenderly caring for his lambs? Does God live far away in the heavens ... or does God abide in intimate communion with people on Earth?

In your journal, list all the names and attributes of God you can think of: Father/Mother, Shepherd, Guide, Comforter, Savior, Teacher, Everlasting One, Provider, Friend ...

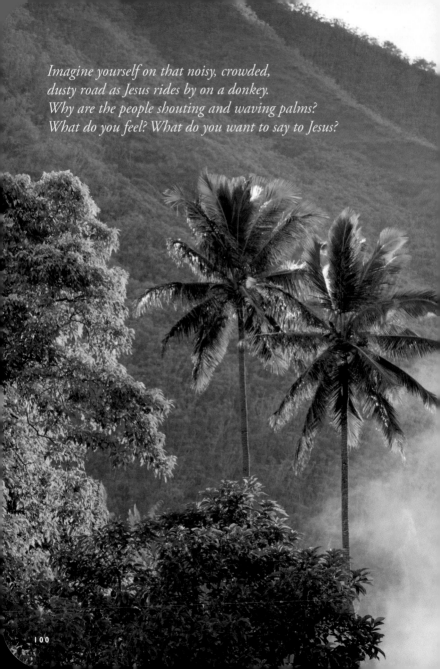

Imagine yourself on that noisy, crowded,
dusty road as Jesus rides by on a donkey.
Why are the people shouting and waving palms?
What do you feel? What do you want to say to Jesus?

PALM TREE

THE GREAT CROWD ... HEARD THAT JESUS WAS ON HIS WAY TO JERUSALEM. THEY TOOK PALM BRANCHES AND WENT OUT TO MEET HIM, SHOUTING,
"HOSANNA!"
"BLESSED IS HE WHO COMES IN THE NAME OF THE LORD!"
"BLESSED IS THE KING OF ISRAEL!"
JOHN 12:12-13 NIV

People greeted Jesus as a political leader who would overthrow the cruel Roman rule. Instead, Jesus came as the promised spiritual Messiah, offering forgiveness for sins and new life. Jesus must have felt alone and misunderstood in that crowd, aware that in a few short days many of the same people would be shouting, "Crucify him!"

Many Christian churches distribute palm branches to remember Jesus on Palm Sunday. The palms are later burned and the ashes used on the following Ash Wednesday to symbolize mortality and penance. Congregations are encouraged to remember Christ's sacrificial death on the cross, celebrate his resurrection, and look expectantly for his second coming. At the end of the Bible, people from every nation raise palm branches to honor Jesus:

THERE BEFORE ME WAS A GREAT MULTITUDE THAT NO ONE COULD COUNT, FROM EVERY NATION, TRIBE, PEOPLE AND LANGUAGE, STANDING BEFORE THE THRONE AND IN FRONT OF THE LAMB. THEY WERE WEARING WHITE ROBES AND WERE HOLDING PALM BRANCHES IN THEIR HANDS. AND THEY CRIED OUT IN A LOUD VOICE: "SALVATION BELONGS TO OUR GOD, WHO SITS ON THE THRONE, AND TO THE LAMB [JESUS.]"
REV. 7:9-10 NIV

In ancient times, palm branches symbolized goodness, victory, and peace. They were often depicted on coins and important buildings. Solomon had palm branches carved into the walls and doors of the temple and overlaid with gold.

SEE KINGS 6:29-35

PEACE

Peace of the running wave to you,
Deep peace of the flowing air to you,
Deep peace of the quiet earth to you,
Deep peace of the shining stars to you,
Deep peace of the Son of Peace to you, forever.

-Celtic Oral Tradition

The early Celts living in Ireland and Scotland
firmly believed that God inhabits all of
creation—water, air, earth, and sky. Living
and working outdoors in God's creation, they
recognized the "Son of Peace" as the source
of deep, abiding peace—even in the midst of
chaos.

*Many are experiencing unsettling times, swimming in
tides of change and uncertainty, filled with fears and
anxiety.*

*In the midst of these circumstances, what needs to
happen for you to experience God's "deep peace" within?*

THOSE OF STEADFAST MIND YOU KEEP IN PEACE—
IN PEACE BECAUSE THEY TRUST IN YOU. TRUST IN THE
LORD FOREVER.

Is. 26:3-4 NRSV

CAST ALL
YOUR ANXIETY
ON [GOD],
BECAUSE HE
CARES FOR
YOU.

I PETER 5:7 NRSV

PELICAN

Pelicans frequent inland and coastal waters and feed principally on fish, catching them at or near the water surface. There are several species of pelicans, but all have the familiar elastic throat pouch used to catch fish. They are social birds and typically travel in flocks, often strung out in a line.

An ancient legend said that during famine a mother pelican wounded herself by striking her breast with her beak in order to feed her dying young with her own blood. While saving her young, she sacrificed her own life. Given this tradition, we can see why early Christians adopted the pelican to symbolize Jesus Christ, portraying it in Christian murals, paintings, frescos, and stained glass. As the mother pelican shed her blood that her young might live, Christ also shed His blood on the cross as atonement for the sins of the world. Christ continues to feed Christians on their pilgrim journey with His body and blood in the sacramental holy Eucharist.

How might the pelican image move you to show the same self-giving love toward others?

PERIL ON THE SEA

Eternal Father, Strong to save,
Whose arm hath bound the restless
wave,
Who bid'st the mighty Ocean deep
Its own appointed limits keep;
O hear us when we cry to thee,
for those in peril on the sea.
O Christ! Whose voice the waters heard
And hushed their raging at Thy word,
Who walked'st on the foaming deep,
and calm amidst its rage didst sleep;
Oh hear us when we cry to Thee
For those in peril on the sea!
Most Holy spirit! Who didst brood
Upon the chaos dark and rude,
And bid its angry tumult cease,
And give, for wild confusion, peace;
Oh, hear us when we cry to Thee
For those in peril on the sea!
O Trinity of love and power!
Our brethren shield in danger's hour;
From rock and tempest, fire and foe,
Protect them wheresoe'er they go;
Thus evermore shall rise to Thee,
Glad hymns of praise from land and sea.

-William Whiting, Navy Hymn

*Pray for those who serve their country in
the armed forces.*

*Pray for health and safety, for comfort and com-
panionship, for courage and fortitude
to make wise choices.*

*Pray for protection against enemies,
both of the flesh and the spirit.*

Though our mouths were full of song as the sea,
and our tongues of exultation as the multitude of its waves,
and our lips of praise as the wide-extended firmament;

Though our eyes shone with light like the sun and the moon,
and our hands were spread forth like the eagles of heaven,
and our feet were swift as hinds;

We should still be unable to thank Thee and to Bless Thy name,
O God our God and God of our fathers and mothers,
For one thousandth or one ten thousandth part of the bounties
which Thou hast bestowed upon our fathers and mothers and upon us.

-Hebrew Morning Service, amplified

PRAISE

LORD, OUR LORD, HOW
MAJESTIC IS YOUR NAME IN
ALL THE EARTH!
YOU HAVE SET YOUR GLORY IN
THE HEAVENS ...
WHEN I CONSIDER YOUR
HEAVENS, THE WORK OF YOUR
FINGERS,
   THE MOON AND THE STARS,
WHICH YOU HAVE SET IN PLACE,
WHAT IS MANKIND THAT YOU ARE
MINDFUL OF THEM,
   HUMAN BEINGS THAT YOU CARE
FOR THEM?
... YOU MADE THEM RULERS OVER
THE WORKS OF YOUR HANDS;
   YOU PUT EVERYTHING UNDER
THEIR FEET:
... THE BIRDS IN THE SKY, AND
THE FISH IN THE SEA, ALL THAT
SWIM THE PATHS OF THE SEAS.

PSALM 8 NIV

God is the center of all creation,
not humankind. The psalmist is
aware of a true reciprocity: as
we care for creation, we realize
that God, through creation, cares
for us. Seeing creation as God's
gift helps us understand our
vocation and worth as human
beings. With the psalmist, we can
exclaim with wonder and praise.

*Write your own psalm of praise
for creation.*

PRAYER

Prayer is larger than any of us. It is less a question of bringing prayer into our hearts than of bringing our hearts into prayer; not drawing water from the sea to fill a bath, but being immersed in an immense ocean and becoming one with it.

Prayer is not controlled. We are the ones controlled, called upon to submit to a mysterious inward process, to be carried beyond ourselves without ever knowing clearly what carries us or where we are going.

-Michael Casey

Too often our prayers are monologues talking at God, launching our spiritual shopping lists heavenward. Richard Foster reminds us, however, that God is not our "cosmic bellhop." When we keep silent, we realize that prayer is more about listening than talking. We are completely dependent on God to initiate even our love and thirst for God … a desire and longing that only God can fill.

Our only response to the work of God's Spirit within is to be still and present to the ongoing conversation already deep within us. Like in any relationship, such intimacy cannot be forced or contrived and it requires time and commitment to grow and flourish.

Is your prayer life more about talking or listening?

How do you bring your heart into prayer, becoming immersed and one with it?

The Spirit helps us in our weakness: for we do not know how to pray as we ought, but that very Spirit intercedes with sighs too deep for words.

Romans 8:26
NRSV

PROTECTION

Bᴜᴛ ɴᴏᴡ ᴛʜᴜs sᴀʏs ᴛʜᴇ LORD,
   ʜᴇ ᴡʜᴏ ᴄʀᴇᴀᴛᴇᴅ ʏᴏᴜ, O Jᴀᴄᴏʙ,
   ʜᴇ ᴡʜᴏ ꜰᴏʀᴍᴇᴅ ʏᴏᴜ, O Isʀᴀᴇʟ:
Dᴏ ɴᴏᴛ ꜰᴇᴀʀ, ꜰᴏʀ I ʜᴀᴠᴇ ʀᴇᴅᴇᴇᴍᴇᴅ ʏᴏᴜ;
  I ʜᴀᴠᴇ ᴄᴀʟʟᴇᴅ ʏᴏᴜ ʙʏ ɴᴀᴍᴇ, ʏᴏᴜ ᴀʀᴇ ᴍɪɴᴇ.
Wʜᴇɴ ʏᴏᴜ ᴘᴀss ᴛʜʀᴏᴜɢʜ ᴛʜᴇ ᴡᴀᴛᴇʀs,
I ᴡɪʟʟ ʙᴇ ᴡɪᴛʜ ʏᴏᴜ;
  ᴀɴᴅ ᴛʜʀᴏᴜɢʜ ᴛʜᴇ ʀɪᴠᴇʀs, ᴛʜᴇʏ sʜᴀʟʟ ɴᴏᴛ
ᴏᴠᴇʀᴡʜᴇʟᴍ ʏᴏᴜ;
ᴡʜᴇɴ ʏᴏᴜ ᴡᴀʟᴋ ᴛʜʀᴏᴜɢʜ ꜰɪʀᴇ ʏᴏᴜ sʜᴀʟʟ
ɴᴏᴛ ʙᴇ ʙᴜʀɴᴇᴅ,
  ᴀɴᴅ ᴛʜᴇ ꜰʟᴀᴍᴇ sʜᴀʟʟ ɴᴏᴛ ᴄᴏɴsᴜᴍᴇ ʏᴏᴜ.
Fᴏʀ I ᴀᴍ ᴛʜᴇ LORD ʏᴏᴜʀ Gᴏᴅ,
  ᴛʜᴇ Hᴏʟʏ Oɴᴇ ᴏꜰ Isʀᴀᴇʟ, ʏᴏᴜʀ Sᴀᴠɪᴏʀ.

Isᴀɪᴀʜ 43:1-3ᴀ ɴʀsᴠ

Sometimes storms in our life are fierce, skies are
grey, and God seems absent. Wind and seas buffet
our lives, tossing us to and fro with no apparent
purpose. There are no promises of deliverance
from struggle and conflict, but God does promise
to be with us through them. When we face
overwhelming waves, we are called to flow with
them in faith and hope, not to sink in helplessness.

Henri Nouwen offers this word of hope:

*Life is God's initiative and can end or change suddenly,
unexpectedly, and unpredictably. When we humans are
ready to give up hope and resign ourselves to inevitability,
God intervenes and reveals completely new beginnings. The
resurrection of Jesus is God's sign breaking through every
form of human fatalism and despair. In every critical event,
there is an opportunity for God to act creatively and reveal
a deeper truth than what we see on the surface of things.
God also can turn around critical incidents and seemingly
hopeless situations in our lives and reveal light in darkness.*

Pray for God's peace in troubled times, joy in the midst of pain,
hope when tempted to despair,
and faith when God seems silent. Be confident that God has
also suffered and overcome,
and that God cares and loves you very much.

PURPOSE

God is working his purpose out
as year succeeds to year:
God is working his purpose out,
and the time is drawing near …
All we can do is done in vain
unless God blesses the deed;
vainly we hope for the harvest-tide
till God gives life to the seed;
yet nearer and nearer draws the time,
the time that shall surely be,
when the earth shall be filled
with the glory of God
as the waters cover the sea.

-Arthur Ainger

God's kingdom is coming! In our speaking and
in our serving, we will be its messengers, but
God alone "gives life to the seed." Only God
knows when it will happen and what it will look
like, but we can let God's light shine through us
and look forward to the day when "every knee
shall bow and every tongue shall give praise to
God." (ROMANS 4:11 NRSV)

FOR THE EARTH WILL BE FULL OF THE
KNOWLEDGE OF THE LORD, AS THE WATERS
COVER THE SEA.

ISAIAH 11:9 NRSV

This prophetic assurance came when
oppression was at its heaviest and God's purpose
seemed obscure. Where is your trust? your hope?

I KNOW THAT YOU CAN
DO ALL THINGS, AND
THAT NO PURPOSE
OF YOURS CAN BE
THWARTED.

JOB 42:2 NRSV

WE KNOW THAT
ALL THINGS WORK
TOGETHER FOR GOOD
FOR THOSE WHO
LOVE GOD, WHO ARE
CALLED ACCORDING TO
HIS PURPOSE.

ROMANS 8:28 NRSV

IT IS GOD WHO IS AT
WORK IN YOU BOTH
TO WILL AND TO
WORK FOR HIS GOOD
PLEASURE.

PHIL. 2:13 NRSV

SALTY WATER

In the Sermon on the Mount, Jesus challenged the disciples to be like salt:

YOU ARE THE SALT OF THE EARTH; BUT IF SALT HAS LOST ITS TASTE, HOW CAN ITS SALTINESS BE RESTORED? IT IS NO LONGER GOOD FOR ANYTHING, BUT IS THROWN OUT AND TRAMPLED UNDERFOOT.

MATTHEW 5:13 NRSV

Do you remember the first time you tasted the saltiness of the sea? Even if you'd been warned, it was still probably quite surprising!

Salt is used for flavoring and as a preservative. If seasoning has lost its flavor, it has no value. Likewise, if Christians assimilate too much into the world around them, they are no longer effective in doing God's work. To be useful in God's Kingdom, Jesus challenges his disciples to make every effort to affect others in positive ways. Just as seasoning brings out the best flavor in foods, we are not to blend in with everyone else, but to contribute zest and hope to everyone around us. We are called to be no less than "the salt of the earth" in word and deed.

Are your relationships "salty"?

Would those you live with say your speech is "seasoned with salt," full of grace and encouragement?

WHEN WE SPEAK, WE ARE TO BE KIND, RESPECTFUL,
AND COURTEOUS, "LET YOUR SPEECH ALWAYS BE GRACIOUS,
SEASONED WITH SALT, SO THAT YOU MAY KNOW HOW YOU OUGHT
TO ANSWER EVERYONE."

COLOSSIANS 4:6 NRSV

SAND

To see a World in a Grain of Sand
And a Heaven in a Wild Flower,
Hold Infinity in the palm of your hand
And eternity in an hour …

-William Blake

Few know how to hold infinity in the palm of our hands; most feel lucky to just hold it together until the end of the day. Our attention is lost in the endless blur of busyness, noise, and worry that make up modern life.

Sometimes, for the briefest moment, we sense there is more to life, but those moments usually pass amidst the daily chaos. Yet even in everyday reality, we can experience moments of transcendent beauty and inspiration when the smallest thing exposes deep truth. Like viewing a grain of sand reveals the whole world in a kind of mystical vision, viewing a wildflower or holding an intricate seashell can transport us to catch a glimpse of heaven.

The sacred can be found in the mundane, the profound in the prosaic, but only if we practice *noticing*. We pass hundreds of natural miracles every day that are simply waiting to be seen and enjoyed.

When have you seen the enormity of God's love in a small piece of creation?

Look for glimpses of God's handiwork in everyday miracles.

SAND AND ROCK

EVERYONE WHO HEARS THESE WORDS OF MINE AND ACTS ON THEM WILL BE LIKE A WISE MAN WHO BUILT HIS HOUSE ON ROCK. THE RAIN FELL, THE FLOODS CAME, AND THE WINDS BLEW AND BEAT ON THAT HOUSE, BUT IT DID NOT FALL, BECAUSE IT HAD BEEN FOUNDED ON ROCK. AND EVERYONE WHO HEARS THESE WORDS OF MINE AND DOES NOT ACT ON THEM WILL BE LIKE A FOOLISH MAN WHO BUILT HIS HOUSE ON SAND. THE RAIN FELL, AND THE FLOODS CAME, AND THE WINDS BLEW AND BEAT AGAINST THAT HOUSE, AND IT FELL—AND GREAT WAS ITS FALL!

MATTHEW 7:24-27 NRSV

You have probably observed both kinds of houses—one built on sand and one built on rock. The news media exposes the damage from fierce storm surges that rip sand from pilings, causing beachfront homes to tumble into the sea. These raging storms are as inevitable as the tide, yet some foolish builders still invest their time and resources in elaborate exteriors—without providing a firm foundation.

The wise man's house represents a life transformed by grace, built on the firm foundation of Jesus Christ. We are called to a committed relationship with Christ, not simply a profession with no actions behind the words.

Sketch a house being battered by wind and waves. In what ways does this image illustrate your own life?

What stormy trials are raging against you? Do you feel yourself faltering? Is Christ your sure foundation, your solid rock?

On Christ the Solid Rock I Stand
My hope is built on nothing less
Than Jesus' blood and righteousne[ss]
I dare not trust the sweetest frame
But wholly trust in Jesus' Name.

On Christ the solid Rock I stand,
All other ground is sinking sand;
All other ground is sinking sand.

When darkness seems to hide His [face]
I rest on His unchanging grace.
In every high and stormy gale,
My anchor holds within the veil.

His oath, His covenant, His bloo[d]
Support me in the whelming floo[d]
When all around my soul gives w[ay]
He then is all my Hope and Stay.

-Edward Mote

Be doers of the
word, and not
merely hearers
who deceive
themselves.

James 1:22 NRSV

Hold a delicate sand dollar in your hand
and inspect its intricate design.
Never remove a live specimen (still fuzzy and brown),
but return it to the sea.

SAND DOLLAR

Sand dollars are sea urchins that abound in shallow coastal waters. Sticking out from five top surface holes, tube feet are used for breathing and eating. The mouth is found on the back of the shell, taking in tiny aquatic organisms where five interior jaws (the "doves") crush the food. Small spines cover the body and help it wiggle through the sandy water. When tossed ashore after storms or high tides, they resemble a fuzzy brown cookie, about 2 to 4 inches wide. Their dried circular skeleton looks like a large, white coin and is often used for decoration and to tell the story of Jesus' life:

The legend of the Sand dollar that I would like to tell
Of the birth and death of Jesus, found in this lovely shell.

If you examine closely, you'll see that you find here
Four nail holes and a fifth one, made by a Roman's spear.

On one side the Easter lily, its center is the star
That appeared unto the shepherds, and led them from afar.

The Christmas poinsettia, etched on the other side
Reminds us of His birthday, our happy Christmastide.

Now break the center open, and here you will release
The five white doves awaiting to spread good will and peace.

This simple little symbol, Christ left for you and me
To help us spread His Gospel, through all eternity.

-Author Unknown

"*The further I wake into this life, the more I realize that God is everywhere and the extraordinary is waiting quietly beneath the skin of all that is ordinary. Light is in both the broken bottle and the diamond, and music is in both the flowing violin and the water dripping from the drainage pipe. Yes, God is under the porch as well as on top of the mountain, and joy is in both the front row and the bleachers, if we are willing to be where we are.*" -Mark Nepo

SANDPIPER

Sandpipers are usually found scurrying on the edge of the shore, searching for their next meal. Their long legs and sensitive bills allow the birds to feel the mud and sand as they probe for prey. Heads down, they maintain constant vigil, employing all their senses to discover what each new wave may bring.

Adults are often too distracted by competing interests to be focused and attentive in the present moment. Dr. Rachel Remen cautions, "Life offers its wisdom generously. Everything teaches. Not everyone learns. Life asks of us the same thing we have been asked in every class: 'Stay awake.' 'Pay attention.' But paying attention is no simple matter. It requires us not to be distracted by expectations, past experiences, labels, and masks. It asks that we not jump to early conclusions and that we remain open to surprise."

Poet Mary Oliver also affirms the importance of paying attention:

"Ten times a day something happens to me like this—some strengthening throb of amazement—some good sweet empathetic ping and swell. This is the first, the wildest and the wisest thing I know: that the soul exists and is built entirely out of attentiveness."

What common distractions are you aware of? How can you live more in the present moment?

SCALLOP SHELL

THE LORD WILL WATCH OVER YOUR COMING AND GOING BOTH NOW AND FOREVERMORE. PSALM 121:8 NIV

The scallop shell first became associated with the apostle Saint James through legends in the Middle Ages telling of James' mission to Spain and burial at Compostela. These legends initiated the ancient pilgrimage route, the Way of St. James, Camino de Santiago. James appears in early paintings as a pilgrim, wearing a scallop shell on his wide-brimmed hat, cloak, or staff.

The scallop shell is found on roads, buildings, and sidewalks, marking the path for pilgrims all across northern Spain. Some are broken, some stolen as souvenirs, some are simple, some very elaborate and beautiful. One traveler reflected, "In all their variations, they marked the route for hundreds of miles. They reminded all of us pilgrims that in the midst of a world both beautiful and broken there are signs to help lead us forward, sometimes right under our feet."

In ancient times the shells indicated the status of pilgrims to the outside world, according them special privileges and hospitality along the way. Pilgrims carried a shell with them to present at churches, castles, and inns where they would be given as much food as they could pick up with one scoop. Thus, even the poorest households could extend charity without being overburdened.

The grooves in the scallop come together at a single point at the tip of the shell. This often represents the various routes pilgrims travel, eventually arriving at their single destination, the tomb of St. James. Since scallop shells are common on the shores of Galicia, returning home with one proved the pilgrims had accomplished their goal.

Pilgrims traditionally return home with a token to remind them of their experience.
Choose a shell to symbolize your journey on this Pilgrim Walk.

Give me my scallop shell of quiet;
My staff of faith to walk upon;
My scrip of joy, immortal diet;
My bottle of salvation;
My gown of glory (hope's true gage)
And then I'll take my pilgrimage.

-Sir Walter Raleigh

BROTHERS AND SISTERS, WHENEVER YOU FACE TRIALS
OF ANY KIND, CONSIDER IT NOTHING BUT JOY,
BECAUSE YOU KNOW THAT THE TESTING OF YOUR
FAITH PRODUCES ENDURANCE; AND LET ENDURANCE
HAVE ITS FULL EFFECT, SO THAT YOU MAY BE MATURE
AND COMPLETE, LACKING IN NOTHING.

JAMES 1:2-4 NRSV

SEA GLASS

Ardent collectors of sea glass often hike or boat long distances to find the best sites for "mermaid's tears". Beachcombers look among the pebbles and shells to discover these frosted beach jewels, especially during the first low tide after a storm. It takes over thirty years of wave action and high water pH to pit the surfaces and smooth the edges of discarded glass from broken bottles, dishes, windows, and even shipwrecks. Sea glass is a "reverse gem." Traditional gemstones like diamonds, rubies, and emeralds are made by nature and refined by humans. Sea glass is originally made by humans but refined by nature into smooth, frosted beach gems. Nature acts like a big rock tumbler recycling our garbage!

The color of sea glass is determined by its original source. The most common colors are green, brown, and blue (from wine, beer, or soft drink bottles). Yellows, oranges, reds and blacks, however, are extremely rare. Artisans incorporate each of these colors of sea glass to craft beautiful pieces of jewelry, stained glass, mosaics, marbles, and other decorative pieces.

Although sea glass was once plentiful, now it is harder to find due to sand replenishment, rising water levels, and increased use of plastics. Today we recognize the fragility of marine life and recycling has discouraged bottles and tableware from being dumped indiscriminately into lakes and oceans.

In the same way that turbulent waters smooth off the rough edges of discarded glass, God uses our troubles to smooth the rough edges of our character, refining our souls to be "mature and complete." It is a slow process and it's sometimes difficult to see results in the chaos and darkness, but we trust that God is indeed at work, creating someone beautiful from the broken shards of our lives.

Find a smooth piece of sea glass and imagine it being tumbled and battered by waves over the years. Keep it as a reminder that God is also refining you, especially when you are suffering. No matter how broken you feel, God uses your trials to smooth the rough edges.

SEAGULLS

God, who hast made seagulls so beautiful.
Cleaving the sky.
so let my service be—
fearless and poised and sure—Teach me to fly!

God who hast taught seagulls to soar and rest
on empty space,
so let me rise to Thee,
dwell in the heavenlies.
Proving Thy grace.

-Amy Carmichael

Found on every continent, numerous species of gulls
breed in marine, freshwater, and terrestrial habitats.
Most gulls are migratory, moving to warmer climates
during the winter and many can be seen soaring high
above beaches on their long journeys.

Seagulls glide for a long time, not by flapping their
wings, but by taking advantage of air currents called
thermals. Warm, rising air from the ground pushes
them upward, helping the gulls to conserve energy.
Unfortunately for gulls, thermals are inconsistent and
not always available. Sun warms the earth or sand,
which then warms the air above it. Some seagulls wait
on the beach until mid-morning, then use the warming
thermals to glide along the beach searching for their
next meal.

Obstruction currents occur when moving air runs into
cliffs or sand dunes and is forced upward. Seagulls can
be seen riding these currents high above cliffs.

*How is God inviting you to soar? What anxieties
can you release and not have to "flap" so much?*

*Pray this poem as your own prayer: "so let my service be—
fearless and poised and sure—Teach me to fly!"*

SEA WALL

Sea walls are constructed to preserve existing shorelines from erosion and storm surge flooding, protecting both lives and property. Shorelines are dynamic; tidal and wave activity can quickly damage coastal areas by drawing sand and sediment into the sea. Sea walls protect the existing coast from drastic change when it is exposed to severe storms and hurricanes.

Environmentalists argue that sea walls disrupt natural coastal processes and destroy the natural habitats of marshes, wetlands, and beaches. Constructing sea walls is often controversial because they are expensive to build and maintain, and they scar the beautiful landscapes they are built to preserve.

People of faith are sometimes like stalwart sea walls or resistant rocky shores. Just as barriers strain to endure the natural elements, insisting on our own way, resisting the push toward compromise and cooperation, take enormous energy. Just as barriers strain to endure the natural elements, insisting on our own way and resisting the push toward compromise and cooperation take enormous energy. A coastline waits patiently, submitting to the unending action of the waves, compliant to the unpredictable forces of nature. The gradual ebb and flow of the tides determines the coastal design, causing sand plants and animals to adapt their habitats as needed.

Like the beach, receiving waves and returning them to the sea, we can choose to patiently and humbly open to God's approach and allow ourselves to be drawn back out in response to the divine power within us. When we are submissive and yielding, God's plan for us can be fulfilled.

Are you more like the resistant rocks or the yielding shore?

How can you be more malleable to the ebb and flow of life's circumstances?

SIMPLICITY

I spend the first days at the beach greedily collecting every beautiful shell I encounter, unable to even glance up for fear of missing another treasure at my feet. But after my pockets are full and the porch and window ledges are covered, I become more selective. I realize that I can only collect a few of all the beautiful shells on the beach—and their beauty is enhanced when they are few.

Anne Morrow Lindbergh observes, "One moon shell is more impressive than three. There is only one moon in the sky ... One sets it apart by itself, ringed around by space—like the island ... For it is only framed in space that beauty blooms ... A tree has significance if one sees it against the empty face of sky. A note in music gains significance from the silences on either side."

Space gives beauty not only to objects, but people and occasions also become more significant. Too often I lack these qualities because empty space is so rare. Worthy causes and important people cram my life, as well as trivial demands. Striving to be useful, important, and influential, I crowd out space necessary for calm and beauty. In acquiring an excess of good things, I realize too late that only one or two would be more significant.

We're tempted to cling to beautiful moments, things, or people, but we cannot possess beauty. By creating space in our lives, moving from acquisitiveness to selectivity, we discover the beauty of one, rather than many. Less is more. Select one shell, put it in a special place, and let it be a reminder of your experience here.

Mostly I walk with my head down,
gathering shells,
looking for the best ones,
staying focused on the task.

I have the collector's penchant
for keeping things organized,
knowing my priorities,
expanding my holdings.

Even when surrounded by beauty
I have a goal:
take it all in,
don't miss a part.

Help me to stop
and take a long, loving look
at just one shell,
at just one smile.

Teach me how
to put a frame around a moment,
to pause reverently,
to see simply.

-Robert M. Hamma

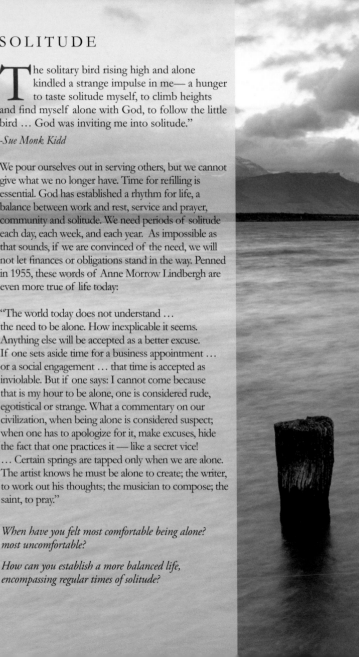

SOLITUDE

The solitary bird rising high and alone
kindled a strange impulse in me— a hunger
to taste solitude myself, to climb heights
and find myself alone with God, to follow the little
bird … God was inviting me into solitude."

-Sue Monk Kidd

We pour ourselves out in serving others, but we cannot
give what we no longer have. Time for refilling is
essential. God has established a rhythm for life, a
balance between work and rest, service and prayer,
community and solitude. We need periods of solitude
each day, each week, and each year. As impossible as
that sounds, if we are convinced of the need, we will
not let finances or obligations stand in the way. Penned
in 1955, these words of Anne Morrow Lindbergh are
even more true of life today:

"The world today does not understand …
the need to be alone. How inexplicable it seems.
Anything else will be accepted as a better excuse.
If one sets aside time for a business appointment …
or a social engagement … that time is accepted as
inviolable. But if one says: I cannot come because
that is my hour to be alone, one is considered rude,
egotistical or strange. What a commentary on our
civilization, when being alone is considered suspect;
when one has to apologize for it, make excuses, hide
the fact that one practices it — like a secret vice!
… Certain springs are tapped only when we are alone.
The artist knows he must be alone to create; the writer,
to work out his thoughts; the musician to compose; the
saint, to pray."

When have you felt most comfortable being alone?
most uncomfortable?

How can you establish a more balanced life,
encompassing regular times of solitude?

Do your little bit of good where you are;
It is those little bits of good put together that
overwhelm the world.

-Desmond Tutu

THE STARFISH

In the morning early,
I saw the folk from the village
combing the sand for starfish
which the waves had washed up
and left vulnerable.

These, the villagers would collect, kill,
and sell for profit.
That was their way.

One morning I rose earlier,
and walked on the sand by the water's edge.

There, in the distance, I saw a solitary figure
who was also looking for starfish.

Whenever he found one alive or even just alive,
he would lift it, kiss it,
and lay it back in the blue water,
there to be revived and to swim again.
That was his way.

Now I get up every morning,
earlier than the villagers,
early as the man.
I, the strong, no longer stretch to survive:
I kneel down to restore the weak.

And I have found,
though some might mock me,
that even far from the seaside,
there are starfish on every street.

-John Bell

How can you "kneel down to restore the weak"?

In a popular version of this story, an old man asks a young girl why she is throwing starfish into the sea. She calmly answers, "So they may live." Skeptical, the old man explains that with thousands of miles of beaches, her small efforts could not possibly make a difference. She listens politely before tossing another starfish into the waves, and replies, "It made a difference for that one!"

STARS

I am fashioned as a galaxy,
Not as a solid substance but a mesh
Of atoms in their far complexity
Forming the pattern of my bone and flesh.
Small solar systems are my eyes,
Muscle and sinew are composed of air.
Like comets flashing through the evening skies
My blood runs, ordered, arrogant, and fair.

Ten lifetimes distant is the nearest star,
And yet within my body, firm as wood,
Proton and electron separate are.
Bone is more fluid than my coursing blood.
What plan had God, so strict and empassioned
When He an island universe my body fashioned?

-Madeleine L'Engle

Ponder the expanse of the stars and galaxies above you and the vastness of the sand beneath you. Imagine the God who created all of this forming your bone and flesh so carefully and intimately. Confess honestly that there are parts of your body you wish were more attractive or functioned more reliably.

Now focus on all that is beautiful and works well to make you just who you are. Be aware of your heartbeat pumping lifeblood and your lungs giving and receiving air without your consciousness. Touch the skin that protects you and your elbow that allows your arm to bend.

Praise God for how you are "fearfully and wonderfully made."

For it was you who
formed my inward
parts;
you knit me together
in my mother's womb.
I praise you, for I am
fearfully and
wonderfully made.
Wonderful are your
works;
that I know very well.
My frame was not
hidden from you;
when I was being made
in secret,
intricately woven in
the depths of the
earth.

Ps. 139: 13-15 NRSV

STEADFAST LOVE

O the deep, deep love of Jesus, vast, unmeasured, boundless, free!
Rolling as a mighty ocean in its fullness over me!
Underneath me, all around me, is the current of Thy love
Leading onward, leading homeward to Thy glorious rest above!

O the deep, deep love of Jesus, spread His praise from shore to shore!
How He loveth, ever loveth, changeth never, nevermore!
How He watches o'er His loved ones, died to call them all His own;
How for them He intercedeth, watcheth o'er them from the throne!

O the deep, deep love of Jesus, love of every love the best!
'Tis an ocean full of blessing, 'tis a haven giving rest!
O the deep, deep love of Jesus, 'tis a heaven of heavens to me;
And it lifts me up to glory, for it lifts me up to Thee!

-S. Trevor Francis

When he wrote this hymn, Trevor Francis was an
English merchant and preacher in the 1800's.
The phrases about water/river/ocean may be
reminiscent of a dark, lonely night when he
crossed a London bridge as a teenager. Staring into
the dark waters of the River Thames below and
contemplating suicide, Francis questioned all he
had believed and the reality of God's love. That
experience led to a spiritual awakening, confirming
that his faith was real and would preserve him
through life's suffering. God's deep, deep love
surrounds us and permeates all that we are and all
that we do.

*Spend some time gazing out at the
vast ocean as you sing this old hymn.*

*Reflect on the limitless, sacrificial,
unchanging nature of God's love for you.*

FOR THE MOUNTAINS MAY DEPART AND THE HILLS BE
REMOVED, BUT MY STEADFAST LOVE SHALL NOT DEPART FROM
YOU, AND MY COVENANT OF PEACE SHALL NOT BE REMOVED,
SAYS THE LORD, WHO HAS COMPASSION ON YOU.

ISAIAH 54:10 NRSV

STORMS

Summer days at the beach can become so hot and the humidity so oppressive that it is almost unbearable. Then, in the afternoon, dark storm clouds gather in the distance, making their way toward you. Soon the storm is raging all around, lightning flashes, thunder rumbles, and the ocean waves are capped in white. The storm passes on, just as quickly as it came. The air is cleansed and the beach has become pleasant and enjoyable once again. The world has changed.

God uses the storms in our lives to clean and purify us, returning us to service with a renewed sense of purpose and trust. Our perspective has changed and we see more clearly.

In the infinity of night skies
in the free flashing of lightning
in whirling elemental winds
you are God.
In the impenetrable mists of dark clouds
in the wild gusts of lashing rain
in the ageless rocks of the sea
you are God and I bless you.
You are in all things
and contained by no thing.
You are the Life of all life
and beyond every name.
You are God and in the eternal mystery
I praise you.

-J. Philip Newell

What storms have you experienced recently?
How might God be using them to give you
new life?

SUN

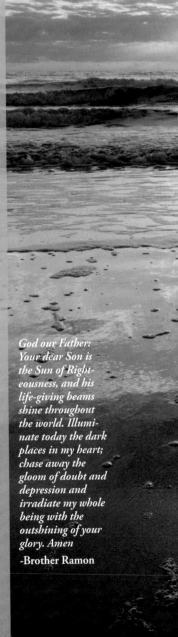

The Sun is gently beneficent, imparting light and warmth, growth and fertility, illumination and glory. The Sun is dangerous, threatening those who live in darkness with dazzling, blinding glory — not because it wills to destroy but because of its very nature. If we are to bear the beams of [God's] love, we must learn gently, but progressively, so that we should more and more be exposed to his glory, and reflect his radiance in this dark world."

-Brother Ramon

Even when clouds or storms block the sun's warm rays, the sun continues to shine. We must take care to prevent our own clouds from obscuring the Light of God. Only God's radiance can illuminate the dark places of our souls and fill us with glory. Just as exposure to the sun's strong rays can be harmful to our bodies, so, too, can exposure to God's light be painful to our souls. Some prefer darkness, choosing not to give up their selfish ways, refusing healthy change. But consider what happens when we are exposed to God's radiance:

ALL OF US, WITH UNVEILED FACES, SEEING THE GLORY OF THE LORD AS THOUGH REFLECTED IN A MIRROR, ARE BEING TRANSFORMED INTO THE SAME IMAGE FROM ONE DEGREE OF GLORY TO ANOTHER; FOR THIS COMES FROM THE LORD, THE SPIRIT.

II COR. 3:18 NRSV

How is God inviting you to reflect God's radiance, goodness, and glory in a dark world?

God our Father: Your dear Son is the Sun of Righteousness, and his life-giving beams shine throughout the world. Illuminate today the dark places in my heart; chase away the gloom of doubt and depression and irradiate my whole being with the outshining of your glory. Amen

-Brother Ramon

SURFING

A spiritual kingdom lies all about us, enclosing us, embracing us, altogether within reach of our inner selves, waiting for us to recognize it. God Himself is here waiting our response to His Presence. This eternal world will come alive to us the moment we begin to reckon upon its reality.

-A.W. Tozer

Walking along the shore at daybreak, we experience moments of calm serenity. Yet more often, the silence makes us aware of the tumult of thoughts, anxieties, and fears lying just below the surface of our consciousness. Our mind's surface is rarely flat and tranquil, like a windless sea.

Sometimes waves are large and tumultuous, at other times small and barely perceptible. Just so, our minds are never completely at rest. Attempting to shut out worldly pressures or suppressing the mind's natural activity creates even more tension and inner struggle. We need to embrace difficult decisions and trials, find meaning in them, and use the energy they create to grow in wisdom and compassion.

John Kabat-Zinn captures this spirit of mindfulness: "You can't stop the waves, but you can learn to surf!" Turbulence diminishes when not continuously agitated. Slowing down and giving our undivided attention to God and God's Word can also replace much of the mind's natural restlessness.

Don't be discouraged if the quiet of your pilgrim walk awakens you to noise within.
Relax. Be still. Inner peace cannot be rushed and is certainly worth waiting for.

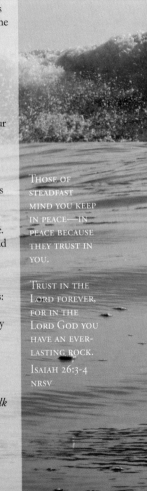

THOSE OF STEADFAST MIND YOU KEEP IN PEACE—IN PEACE BECAUSE THEY TRUST IN YOU.

TRUST IN THE LORD FOREVER, FOR IN THE LORD GOD YOU HAVE AN EVER-LASTING ROCK.

ISAIAH 26:3-4
NRSV

© Tandem/Daniel Kuras

Help me to wait well, Lord, And to live well.
May it be the best waiting I ever do,
hopeful, patient, and full of joy.
And may it be the best living I ever do,
purposeful, peaceful, and pure.

-Eugene Peterson

TIDE POOL

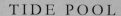

Tide pools teeming with diverse marine life are found along the shore at low tide. Home to hardy invertebrates such as sea stars, sea anemones, mussels, clams, crabs, and algae, tide pools form when the ocean covers the beach twice each day. Tidal pool organisms must adapt to constantly changing environments to survive strong waves and currents, predators, and extreme temperatures. Powerful waves can dislodge mussels and carry them back to sea. Gulls hunt for sea urchins and drop them on rocks to crack them open for their next meal.

Between tides, the smaller pools warm in the midday sun and begin to dry up. Trapped plants and animals must endure fluctuations in water temperature, salinity, and oxygen content. Animals hide under cool, damp rocks and moist seaweeds or burrow in the sand to protect their bodies from drying out before the next high tide arrives to provide refreshment. In the same way, we often feel trapped, exposed to harsh elements, waiting for relief to wash over us. May our waiting and our living be marked by a courageous adaptation to inevitable change.

When we become consumed with what's immediate, focused on survival, we may lose the eternal perspective of life.
How can you experience the abundant life God has for you, both in your waiting and your living?

TIDES

I believe in all that has never yet been
spoken.
I want to free what waits within me
so that what no one has dared to wish for

may for once spring clear
without my contriving.

If this is arrogant, God, forgive me,
but this is what I need to say.
May what I do flow from me like a river,
no forcing and no holding back,
the way it is with children.

Then in these swelling and ebbing currents,
these deepening tides moving out, returning,
I will sing to you as no one ever has,

streaming through widening channels
into the open sea.

-Rainer Maria Rilke

*God has created each of us to be unique, free to
discover our true selves as we discover God,
but sometimes we use this freedom to create a
false persona apart from God.
How can you "free what waits within [you]"?*

*Recall what it was like to play on the sand and
in the waves as a little child.
How might you recover childlike wonder
and play today?*

TRUE SELF

The sea reminds me that most things are temporal, here one moment and gone the next. Yet for that instant they offer great beauty:

This afternoon's tide offers a pentimento of abstract patterns, garnished with shells, stones, and debris. The beach has become a canvas upon which an artist has created a collage, only to change his mind before the paint dries and compose a new overlapping image with the advent of the next wave. I, too, over the years have layered my basic frame, adapting to the demands of a culture, the ideals of a mother, designing and redesigning my persona, and now am finally scraping off the excess to have a glimpse of the original self.

-Joan Anderson

How do I discover my "true self" after a lifetime of adapting to new roles, trying to please or impress others, hiding my fears and inadequacies behind a mask of competency? I catch a "glimpse of my original self," only in the love and mercy of my Creator. In discovering the character of God, I discover my true identity, yielding joy and fulfillment.

Take time to watch the changing tide. What part of your false self is being washed away?

What is coming in to form more of your unique, true self?

TRUST

You call me out upon the waters
  The great unknown where feet may fail
  And there I find You in the mystery
In oceans deep, my faith will stand.
Your grace abounds in deepest waters
Your sovereign hand will be my guide
Where feet may fail and fear surrounds me
You've never failed and You won't start now.
Spirit lead me where my trust is without borders.
Let me walk upon the waters wherever you would call me.
Take me deeper than my feet could ever wander
And my faith will be made stronger in the presence of my Savior.
I will call upon Your Name, Keep my eyes above the waves
When oceans rise my soul will rest in Your embrace
For I am Yours and You are mine.

-Joel Houston, Matt Crocker, and Salomon Lighthelm, "Oceans"

To strengthen our faith and trust, God often calls us deeper than we would ever dare go on our own. God uses our trials to transform us. In a place where "trust is without borders," we learn how utterly dependent we are on God.

WHEN YOU PASS THROUGH THE WATERS, I WILL BE WITH YOU; AND WHEN YOU PASS THROUGH THE RIVERS, THEY WILL NOT SWEEP OVER YOU.

ISAIAH 43:2 NIV

Are you fearful of the unknown future?
Are you facing illness, death, or the loss of a relationship, a job, or a dream?

Are you willing to walk upon the waters wherever God may call you?

The great mystery in terns or turtles
was their inner synchronization with
the changing conditions and ranges
of the planet. That may be why some
of us, still circling, backtracking,
confused by our own directives,
might be envious of them.

-John Hay

THE TURTLE

The sea turtle migrates hundreds of miles from its feeding ground to its nesting beach. Remarkably, adult females return faithfully to nest on the same beach, even within a few hundred yards from where they were born and last nested. Unfortunately, beach erosion, artificial lights, and beach restorations are all affecting turtle migration on once pristine beaches.

We have much to learn from the slow, deliberate behavior of turtles. They persevere by taking small steps to get where they need to go. Even dragging their cumbersome shell with short, ungainly legs, their perseverance can prevail over indolence.

"Slow and steady wins the race," teaches Aesop's fable, "The Tortoise and the Hare." While admirable, the turtle's determination and patience will never win any races against a fast and consistent opponent. The Tortoise accepted a challenge that he couldn't possibly win, but zealously committed to try his best.

The moral of the story could also include the rabbit's arrogant, lazy attitude. The Hare took for granted that he could win; instead of finishing the race, he took a long nap as the resolute Tortoise passed by on his way to the finish line. Fast and consistent can always beat slow and steady, but overconfidence and pride often results in embarrassing failure. Many have strong natural abilities but fail to use them responsibly.

Which animal most represents you this past week? Do you have anything to learn from the slow, persistent Tortoise or the lazy, careless Hare?

UNDERWATER SEA LIFE

Standing on shore, peering over the surface of the water, it's easy to forget the magical, awe-inspiring world below. Unless we don a snorkel and mask or scuba gear, underwater sea life remains a mystery. Scientists estimate that more than half of all life on earth is found under the ocean's surface, yet the dark, cold environment of the deep sea still holds secrets. Rare explorations into the deep have discovered that even without sun and oxygen, life is abundant. Scientists have named and classified around 1.5 million sea species but potentially 50 million more species remain yet to be discovered.

Too often we are reluctant to explore our own depths. Content with what can be seen on the surface of our spiritual life, we neglect the more important solitary, interior life. Results can be easily measured in the exterior life, but we have little or no evidence of progress in the interior sphere. Progress is measured only by God and unseen by all others, including ourselves. This real, lasting work of the godly life is not a matter of adherence to visible standards. Instead, the interior, anguished, solitary act of faith affirms our total subjection to God and God's will in the inmost depths of our being.

WE DO NOT LOSE HEART. THOUGH OUTWARDLY WE ARE WASTING AWAY, YET INWARDLY WE ARE BEING RENEWED DAY BY DAY. FOR OUR LIGHT AND MOMENTARY TROUBLES ARE ACHIEVING FOR US AN ETERNAL GLORY THAT FAR OUTWEIGHS THEM ALL. SO WE FIX OUR EYES NOT ON WHAT IS SEEN, BUT ON WHAT IS UNSEEN, SINCE WHAT IS SEEN IS TEMPORARY, BUT WHAT IS UNSEEN IS ETERNAL.

II CORINTHIANS 4:16-18 NIV

Lord, protect me from seeing momentary troubles or successes as my true reality. Give me abiding faith that you are indeed working in the deep, unseen places of my heart. Fix my eyes on what is of eternal value, that I may not lose heart.

WAITING

O LORD, HOW MANIFOLD ARE YOUR
WORKS! IN WISDOM YOU HAVE MADE
THEM ALL; THE EARTH IS FULL OF
YOUR CREATURES. YONDER IS THE SEA, GREAT
AND WIDE, CREEPING THINGS INNUMERABLE
ARE THERE, LIVING THINGS BOTH SMALL
AND GREAT. THESE ALL LOOK TO YOU TO GIVE
THEM THEIR FOOD IN DUE SEASON; WHEN
YOU GIVE IT TO THEM, THEY GATHER IT UP;
WHEN YOU OPEN YOUR HAND, THEY ARE
FILLED WITH GOOD THINGS.

PSALM 104:24-25, 27-28 NRSV

All of creation waits for God, and what the
animals and birds do unconsciously, God's
people do with reverence and care.
Sea creatures don't worry about the future,
about their health, or about food and shelter.
They bask in the beauty of their world, trusting
by instinct that their needs will be met. Nature
offers a vivid reminder of our relationship to
God. We can depend on God for all our needs.

How can people see me feeding and nurturing the
worm within the dry wood, pasturing the brute
beasts, nourishing the fish in the sea, all the animals
on the earth and the birds in the air, commanding
the sun to shine on the plants and the dew to
fertilize the soil, and not believe that I nourish
them as well, my creatures made in my image and
likeness? As a matter of fact, all this is done by my
goodness to serve them. No matter where they turn,
spiritually and materially they will find nothing but
my deep burning charity and the greatest, gentle,
true, perfect providence.

-Catherine of Siena

Are you patiently trusting God
as you wait for provision?

As you walk, what is troubling you?
Become aware of divine presence in the song of the sea
— and in your own life.

WALKING

I go down to the shore in the morning and depending
on the hour the waves are rolling in or moving out,
and I say, oh, I am miserable,
what shall—
what should I do? And the sea says in its lovely voice:
Excuse me, I have work to do.

-*Mary Oliver*

I have spent countless mornings walking along the shore
asking this very question: *"What shall—what should I do?"*
And all that I hear are the pounding waves, the gulls
crying overhead, and my footsteps. Putting one foot in
front of the other seems to be all that I can do to calm
my restless spirit. I am anxious and I want answers—
now! *What should I do?*

The seashore is in no hurry to answer my insistent query.
In fact, the natural world is excruciatingly slow. Pebbles
are chiseled and smoothed ever so slowly by the
ceaseless caress of wind and waves. Trees inch upward
without our ever noticing. Flattened by hurricanes, dunes
seem to take forever to rebuild, followed ever so slowly
by sea oats and grasses to help anchor the sand until
next time. *"Excuse me, I have work to do,"* they all say.

In *The Quotidian Mysteries*, Kathleen Norris insists that
the "divine presence is revealed even in the meaningless
workings of daily life." So when I don't know what
else to do, I walk and I ponder: *What should I do?* And
I remember God who created me, Christ who renews
me, and the Spirit who enables me to grow in love.
Walking becomes a path to prayer, a reminder that I
am created in the very image of God. Slowly I become
aware of the beauty of my mundane reality. The sun
forms a pink lining behind each feathery cloud. A child
runs to share the treasure in her yellow bucket. My dog
attacks the oncoming wave, then chases it back out to
sea. Laughing, I turn back toward home. I have work
to do.

WAVES

There are nights that are so still
that I can hear the small owl calling
far off and a fox barkingmiles away.
It is then that I liein the lean hours awake
and listeningto the swell born somewhere
in the Atlanticrising and falling, rising and
fallingwave on wave on the long shore
by the village, that is without light
and companionless. And the thought
comes of that other being who is awake,
too,letting our prayers break on him,
not like this for a few hours,
but for days, years, for eternity.

- R. S. Thomas, *The Other*

Imagine being alone in a lightless,
companionless place. Listen to the waves
breaking on the shore. Our prayers are
like the waves, continually pleading. Our
lives are like the waves, continually jumbled
and crashing.
Pray now, marveling at God's mysterious
faithfulness to meet us no matter how far
we stretch. Like the shore, God receives us and
whatever chaos we bring.

He who watches over
Israel [and us] will
neither slumber nor
sleep.

Ps. 121:4 NIV

WHALE

Herman Melville's novel *Moby Dick* considers the merit of the whale's thick blubber: "It is by reason of this cosy blanketing of his body, that the whale is enabled to keep himself comfortable in all weathers, in all seas, times, and tides ... that herein we see the rare virtue of a strong individual vitality, and rare virtue of thick walls, and the rare virtue of interior spaciousness. Oh, man! admire and model thyself after the whale! Do thou, too, remain warm among ice. Do thou, too, live in this world without being of it. Be cool at the equator; keep thy blood fluid at the Pole ... Like the great whale, retain, O man! in all seasons a temperature of thine own."

"Live in this world without being of it." Physically present in the world, enjoying God's good gifts, Christians are called to be holy and set apart, not to adopt worldly values or chase after worldly pleasures. Offering light to those in spiritual darkness, Christians live in such a way that others can see their good deeds and the fruit of God's Spirit in their attitudes and behavior.

Melville challenges us to cultivate the rare virtues of "a strong individual vitality ... thick walls ... and interior spaciousness" found in the adaptable whale.

How might these virtues help you to live more in the world without being conformed to it?

Do not
conformed to this world, but be
transformed by the renewing of your minds, so
that you may discern what is the will of God—
what is good and acceptable and perfect.

Romans 12:1-2 nrsv

WIND AND WAVES

IF ANY OF YOU IS LACKING IN WISDOM, ASK GOD, WHO GIVES TO ALL GENEROUSLY AND UNGRUDGINGLY, AND IT WILL BE GIVEN YOU. BUT ASK IN FAITH, NEVER DOUBTING, FOR THE ONE WHO DOUBTS IS LIKE A WAVE OF THE SEA, DRIVEN AND TOSSED BY THE WIND; FOR THE DOUBTER, BEING DOUBLE-MINDED AND UNSTABLE IN EVERY WAY, MUST NOT EXPECT TO RECEIVE ANYTHING FROM THE LORD.

JAMES 1:5-8 NRSV

Wisdom is not acquired knowledge but the ability to make wise decisions in difficult circumstances. Proverbs describes godly wisdom as practical and relevant to living a right, just, and fair life. (Prov. 1:3) Divine wisdom is not just "common sense," but the ability to be joyful in the midst of trials.   Putting aside skeptical or critical attitudes, we pray confidently, expectant that God will hear our pleas and answer our requests because of God's love and care for us. Of course, God will not answer every casual and selfish request, but will align our desires with divine purposes.

Observe the constant rolling of the ocean waves, subject to the forces of tides, wind, and gravity. When we're not completely convinced that God's way is best, doubt causes us to waver, restless as the ocean waves. When seeking human advice, we reserve the right to disagree and we vacillate between our feelings and others' opinions. But when we seek God's wisdom, we're told to put away all doubts, humbly saying to God, "I believe. Help my unbelief." (Mk. 9:24) To know inner peace, to make prudent decisions, and to stabilize our wavering minds, we're told to ask God in faith for wisdom and trust that God will hear our plea and respond.

As you watch turbulent ocean waves, examine your prayer life. Are you a doubter, double-minded, unstable in all your ways?

Or are you seeking God's wisdom in faith, never doubting God's generous provision?

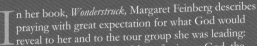

WONDER

In her book, *Wonderstruck,* Margaret Feinberg describes praying with great expectation for what God would reveal to her and to the tour group she was leading: "More than anything, what I long for is our God, the One who bedazzled the heavens and razzle-dazzled the earth, to meet us in such a way during our time in Scotland that we find ourselves awestruck by his goodness and generosity, his provision and presence. I'm praying for pixie dust. I want to leave here with a sense of wonderment as we encounter and experience things only God can do."

How would you have reacted if we'd begun this Pilgrim Walk by "praying for pixie dust"? I may have been skeptical if a tour guide introduced a much-anticipated trip with those words, yet I long to rekindle childlike wonder.

Why do we wait for children before we plan picnics, visit the zoo, build sandcastles, fly kites, catch lightning bugs, carve pumpkins, splash in puddles? Have we outgrown such simple pleasures? When did we lose an unhurried appreciation of small everyday miracles?

When we pray to experience wonder, it changes how we live. We turn our eyes to God who begins to transform us from the inside out. We expect to catch glimpses of God in ways we've never experienced before. Feinberg says, "A prayer for wonder invites you to look for God under, in, and behind every bush." We no longer view friendly encounters as mere chance, but recognize them as divine appointments. We recover childlike expectancy and delight in new discoveries. Best of all, as we discover the wonders of God's creation, we realize that we, too, are "wonder-fully made!" (Ps. 139:14)

Do you long for a renewed sense of wonder?

Ask God for your desires and be prepared for a wonder-filled journey!

WORSHIP

We thank you, holy creator, that you allow us to live surrounded by evidence of your divinity on this island where we find what Saint Francis loved: the endless improvisation of mockingbirds in sculpted bodies of live oaks, the great blue heron in stilted slow motion through jade shadows, a king fisher in its hover and dive, a sandpiper's blurred scurry, pelicans in their elegant ground-effect glides.

Too often we turn our backs, dear God, on you and exile ourselves in favor of phantoms that falsely flatter but you do not forget us, and in your goodness and mercy readily welcome us back to the grace notes of your kingdom that we might be restored and learn once again who we really are.

As Jesus was, we are called to islands of solitude, to vast stores of unused quiet to be with You, to immensities of ocean blue that enlarge our souls and remind us of eternity, and of what passes, but with promise.

When the low sun spreads its orange oil on Bogue Sound, and when the island ripens into darkness, you gift us with bright constellations and infuse us with the mystery of your infinite spaces and the heavens that await us.

And so we come together today under a sun-shafted canopy of maritime forest to receive your Word and join with Saints and Angels in a chorus of praise and thanksgiving that rings through eternity, lifting our voices to magnify you as we say: Holy, holy, holy Lord, God of power and might, heaven and earth are full of your glory. Hosanna in the highest!

-Peter Makuck

Take time to stop, look, and listen to
what is around and within you.
Write your own prayer of praise and
thanksgiving for this moment in this place.

END OF WALK

Has God opened your heart and mind to new expressions of God's love and faithfulness? As you explore God's invitation into a new way of being, remember that other pilgrims join you on the road, sharing stories, tears, laughter, and a God who loves us all.

Whether your pilgrimage requires an arduous journey over a lifetime or a single day spent at the sea, it is an outward expression of an inner movement toward deeper faith and holiness. Pilgrims often return to their familiar surroundings having been changed profoundly. This is sometimes manifest in the recognition of how much we originally missed or took for granted:

We shall not cease from exploration
And the end of all our exploring
Will be to arrive where we started
And know the place for the first time.

-T. S. Eliot

The Iona Community off the southern coast of Scotland remains dedicated to honor and protect the fragile ecosystem of their island. This prayer speaks for all of us traveling the path of God:

O God of the high heavens,
O Christ of the deep earth,
O Spirit of the flowing waters,
O Trinity of love,
You have offered your love to us,
And here we pledge our love to you.
You have been faithful to your people through the ages,
And here we pledge our faithfulness to one another.
You have sustained in love the earth, sea and sky around us,
And here we pledge our sustaining love for creation.
You have identified with the powerless and the weak of the world,
And here we pledge our identification with them.
O God, strengthen us in our desire,
And breathe into our bodies the passion of your love.

INDEX

I Cor. 3:16-17 NRSV, 74-75
I Corinthians 10:13 NIV, 42-43
I John 4:9, 11 NRSV, 64-65
I Kings 6:29-35, 100-101
I Peter 5:7 NRSV, 102-103
I Thess. 2:7-8, 11-12 NIV, 96-97
I Thess. 5:18 NIV , 68-69
II Cor. 3:18 NRSV, 146-147
II Corinthians 4:7 NRSV, 18-19
II Corinthian 4:16-18 NIV, 160-161

A

A.W. Tozer, 148-149
ACKNOWLEDGMENTS, 5
Acts 4:31 NIV, 60-61
Aesop's fable, 158-159
Ainger, Arthur, 114-115
Alexandria, Clement of, 46-47
algae, 84-85
Amanda Arwe, 5
amphibians, 96-97
Amy Carmichael, 68-69, 130-131
anchor , 84-85, 78-79
Anderson, Joan, 154-155
Anne Morrow Lindbergh, 6-7,
134-135, 136-137
Annie Dillard, 28-29
armed forces, 106-107
Arthur Ainger, 114-115
Arwe, Amanda, 5
Ash Wednesday, 100-101
attention, 76-77, 124-125
Augustine, St. of Hippo, 88-89
AUTHORS, 10-11
AWE, 12-13

B

BALANCE, 14-15
Barbara Jones, 5
Bell, John L. , 62-63, 138-139
Beth A. Richardson, 20-21
Betty Skinner, 5
Bjorklund, Mary Sue, 5
Blake, William, 118-119
BOAT, 16-17
Bogue Sound, 174-175
borrowed house, 74-75
Breton Sailor's Prayer, 16-17
Brian D. McLaren, 96-97
broken, 128-129
BROKEN SEASHELLS, 18-19
Brother Ramon, 146-147
Brunton, Paul, 20-21
Buechner, Frederick, 26-27

C

Camara, Helder, 26-27
Camino de Santiago, 126-127
Carmichael, Amy, 68-69, 130-131
Carmichael, Sarah Elizabeth
Hassell, 3
Carmina Gadelica, 90-91
Carson, Rachel, 24-25, 44-45
Cary Slatery, 5
Casey, Michael, 110-111
Catherine of Siena, 34-35, 162-163
CENTERED, 20-21
child, 62-63
Christian symbolism, 78-79
christian symbols, 46-47
Christina Rossetti, 8-9

church, 60-61

Church of the Multiplication, 46-47

Claypool, John, 68-69

Clement of Alexandria, 46-47

clouds, 96-97

Coast Guard Academy, 56-57

Colossians 4:6 NRSV, 116-117

Columba's Bay, 82-83

Come Thou Fount of Every Blessing, 38-39

community ministry, 14-15

CONCH SHELL, 22-23

CONSERVATION, 24-25

Convivio, 72-73

Corrie Ten Boom, 54-55

cosmic bellhop, 110-111

Cowan, Frances Slatery, 5

CREATION, 26-27

CREATIVITY, 28-29

Crocker, Matt, 156-157

Crossley-Holland, Kevin, 32-33

D

Daniel Kuras, 148-149

Dante Alighieri, 72-73

DARING, 30-31

David Gayk, 5

DAWN, 32-33

de Waal, Esther, 90-91

death, 72-73

Deb Hardison, 5

Debbie Henn, 5

Debbie Patrick, 5

DEDICATION, 3

DEEP WATER, 34-35

deliverance, 12-13, 36-37

Denise Levertov, 50-51

Desmond Tutu, 138-139

DESPAIR, 36-37

Dillard, Annie, 28-29

dolphin, 78-79

Donne, John, 80-81

Dorothy Krieg, 5

doubts, 170-171

Drake, Sir Francis, 30-31

DRIFTWOOD, 38-39

DROP IN THE OCEAN, 40-41

E

Eccles. 1:2-9, 14 NRSV, 58-59

Edward Mote, 120-121

Eileen Judice, 5

Eliot, T. S. , 176-177

Elizabeth Dodson Gray, 6-7

Emily Huff, 5

END OF WALK, 176-177

ESCAPE, 42-43

Esther de Waal, 90-91

ETERNITY, 44-45

Eugene Peterson, 150-151

Exodus 13:21-22 NIV, 70-71

F

Faber, Frederick W., 88-89

Feinberg, Margaret, 172-173

Fiona Martin, 82-83

FISH, 46-47

fish and loaves, 62-63

FISHERMAN, 48-49

FLOATING, 50-51

FOOTPRINTS IN THE SAND, 52-53

FORGIVENESS, 54-55

form , 96-97

Foster, Richard, 110-111

Frances Slatery Cowan, 5

Francis Drake, Sir, 30-31

Francis, Trevor S. , 142-143

Frederick Buechner, 26-27

Frederick Martin Lehman, 64-65

Frederick W. Faber, 88-89

FREEDOM, 56-57

Fulk, Martha Ann, 5

FUTILITY, 58-59

G

Galicia, 126-127

Gayk, David, 5

GEESE, 60-61

GENEROSITY, 62-63

Georganne Shultz Hassell, 5

Gift From The Sea, 6-7, 134-135, 136-137

glass, 128-129

glory, 114-115

GOD'S LOVE, 64-65

God's temple, 74-75
Goodrum, Nancy, 5
Gordon B. Hinckley, 86-87
GRATITUDE, 66-67
gravitational pull, 92-93
Gray, Elizabeth Dodson, 6-7
GREY SEAS, 68-69
GUIDANCE, 70-71
gulls, 130-131

H

Hamilton-Poore, Sam, 50-51, 138-139
Hamma, Robert M. , 134-135
Hanh, Thich Nhat, 6-7
HARBOR, 72-73
Hardison, Deb, 5
Hassell, Georganne Shultz, 5
Hassell, Paul, 11
Hassell, Susanne Vanzant, 10, 191
Hay, John, 158-159
Heart-in-Waiting, 32-33
Hebrew Morning Service, 108-109
Hebrews 6:19 NIV, 78-79
Hebrews 6:19 NIV, 84-85
Hebrews 11:1 NRSV, 92-93
Helder Camara, 26-27
Henn, Debbie , 5
Henri Nouwen, 112-113
Henry Wadsworth Longfellow, 86-87
Herman Melville, 168-169
HERMIT CRAB, 74-75
HERON, 76-77
Hillsong United, 156-157
Hinckley, Gordon B, 86-87
holdfast, 84-85
Holland, Kevin Crossley, 32-33
HOLY PATHS, 191
HOPE, 78-79
house on rock, 120-121
house on sand, 120-121
Houston, Joel, 156-157
HOW TO USE THIS FIELD GUIDE, 6-7
hub, 20-21

Huff, Emily, 5
hungry crowd, 62-63
Huston Smith, 6-7
interior life, 160-161
Iona, 82-83
Iona Community, 176-177
Iona poem, 176-177
Irish farewell prayer, 70-71
Isaiah 9:2 NRSV, 86-87
Isaiah 26:3-4 NRSV, 148-149
Isaiah 26:3-4 NRSV, 102-103
Isaiah 40:11 NIV, 96-97
Isaiah 43:1-3 NRSV, 112-113
Isaiah 43:2 NIV, 156-157
Isaiah 43:4 NRSV, 48-49
Isaiah 46:4 NIV, 52-53
Isaiah 54:10 NRSV, 142-143
ISLAND, 80-81

J

J. Philip Newell, 94-95, 144-145
James 1:2-4 NRSV, 128-129
James 1:5-8 NRSV, 170-171
James 1:22 NRSV, 120-121
Jeanne Maxwell, 5
Jennifer Smith, 5
Jeremiah 23:23-24 NRSV, 92-93
Joan Anderson, 154-155
Job 9:5-10 NIV, 44-45
Job 11:7-9 NIV, 3
Joel Houston, 156-157
John 12:12-13 NIV, 100-101
John 13:34-35 NRSV, 46-47
John 17:4 NRSV, 40-41
John 21:9, 12, 14 NRSV, 82-83
John Claypool, 68-69
John Donne, 80-81
John Hay, 158-159
John Kabat-Zinn, 148-149
John L. Bell, 62-63, 138-139
John Masefield, 56-57
Jonah, 36-37
Jonah 2:1-10 The Message, 36-37
Jones, Barbara, 5
Jordan River, 12-13
Joseph Smith, 86-87
JOURNEY, 82-83
Judice, Eileen, 5

Kabat-Zinn, John, 148-149
Kathleen Norris, 164-165
KELP, 84-85
Kevin Crossley-Holland, 32-33
Kidd, Sue Monk, 136-137
Krieg, Dorothy, 5
Kuras, Daniel, 148-149

L

L'Engle, Madeleine, 140-141
Legend of the Sand Dollar, 122-123
Lehman, Frederick Martin, 64-65
Levertov, Denise, 50-51
light and darkness, 112-113
light in darkness, 36-37
Lighthelm, Salomon, 156-157
LIGHTHOUSE, 86-87
Lindbergh, Anne Morrow, 6-7,
134-135, 136-137
Lisa Murray, 5
loaves and fishes, 62-63
long life, 58-59
Longfellow, Henry Wadsworth,
86-87
Luci Shaw, 22-23
Luke 5:4 NRSV, 34-35
Luke 6:12-13, 17-18 NIV, 14-15
Lunetta, Patricia A., 76-77

M

Madeleine L'Engle, 140-141
Magi, 70-71
Makuck, Peter, 174-175
Malachi 4:2, 146-147
Margaret Feinberg, 172-173
Mark 4:37-41 NRSV, 16-17
Mark 9:24, 170-171
Mark Nepo, 124-125
Martha Ann Fulk, 5
Martin, Fiona, 82-83
Mary Oliver, 96-97, 124-125,
164-165
Mary Stevenson, 52-53
Mary Sue Bjorklund, 5
Masefield, John, 56-57
Matt Crocker, 156-157
Matthew 2:9-12 NIV, 70-71
Matthew 4:19 NRSV, 48-49

Matthew 5:13 NRSV, 116-117
Matthew 7:24-27 NRSV, 120-121
Maxwell, Jeanne, 5
McDonald, Rebecca Ramsey, 5
McLaren, Brian D., 96-97
Melville, Herman, 168-169
MERCY, 88-89
Micah 7:18-19 NIV, 54-55
Michael Casey, 110-111
Moby Dick, 168-169
Monson, Thomas S. , 86-87
MOON, 90-91
MOON AND TIDES, 92-93
Moses, 42-43
Mote, Edward, 120-121
Mother Teresa, 40-41
Mt. Sinai, 12-13
multitasking, 20-21
Murray, Lisa, 5

N

Nancy Goodrum, 5
nature's wisdom, 76-77
Naval Hymn, 106-107
Nepo, Mark, 124-125
Newell, J. Philip, 94-95, 144-145
NIGHT, 94-95
no fishing, 54-55
Norris, Kathleen, 164-165
Nouwen, Henri, 112-113
nurture, 96-97

O

Oceans, 156-157
Oliver, Mary, 96-97, 124-125,
164-165
OPSREYS, 96-97
ORIGINALITY, 96-97

P

palm branches, 100-101
Palm Sunday, 100-101
PALM TREE, 100-101
Patricia A. Lunetta, 76-77
Patrick, Debbie, 5
Patrick, George, 5
Paul Brunton, 20-21
Paul Hassell, 11

paying attention, 76-77, 124-125
PEACE, 102-103
peace, 60-61
PELICAN, 104-105
perfection, 18-19
PERIL ON THE SEA, 106-107
Peter Makuck, 174-175
Peterson, Eugene, 150-151
Philip Newell, 94-95, 144-145
Pilgrim Walk by the Sea, 191
Pilgrim Walk in the City, 191
Pilgrim Walk in the Woods, 191
pixie dust, 172-173
pollution, 24-25
Poore, Sam Hamilton, 50-51,
138-139
PRAISE, 108-109
PRAYER, 110-111
PROTECTION, 112-113
Prov. 1:3, 170-171
provision, 162-163
Psalm 8 NIV, 108-109
Psalm 27:1 NRSV, 86-87
Psalm 37:23-24 NRSV, 52-53
Psalm 42:7, 34-35
Psalm 46:1 NRSV, 72-73
Psalm 77:6 NRSV, 94-95
Psalm 96:1, 11 NRSV, 26-27
Psalm 104:24-25, 27-28 NRSV,
162-163
Psalm 107 NRSV, 66-67
Psalm 114 NIV, 12-13
Psalm 121:8 NIV, 126-127
Psalm 139:13-15 NRSV, 140-141
Psalm 139:14, 172-173
Psalm 139:23-24 NRSV, 38-39
PURPOSE, 114-115

Q

Quotidian Mysteries, 164-165

R

R. S. Thomas, 8-9, 166-167
Rachel Carson, 24-25, 44-45
Rachel Remen, 124-125
Rainer Maria Rilke, 152-153
Raleigh, Sir Walter, 126-127
Ramon, Brother, 146-147

raptors, 96-97
Rebecca Ramsey McDonald, 5
Red Sea, 12-13, 42-43
relationships, 116-117
Remen, Dr. Rachel, 124-125
rescue, 42-43
resistant, 132-133
Rev. 7:9-10 NIV, 100-101
Rev. William Whiting, 106-107
Richard Foster, 110-111
Richardson, Beth A, 20-21
Rilke, Rainer Maria, 152-153
Robert M. Hamma, 134-135
Robert Robinson, 38-39
Robinson, Robert, 38-39
Romans 8:26 NRSV, 110-111
Romans 8:26, 34-35
Romans 12:1-2 NRSV, 168-169
Rossetti, Christina, 8-9
rough edges, 128-129

S

S. Trevor Francis, 142-143
sacrifice, 104-105
safe haven, 72-73
sailing vessel, 56-57
Sailor's Prayer, 16-17
salamanders, 96-97
Salomon Lighthelm, 156-157
SALTY WATER   , 116-117
Sam Hamilton-Poore, 50-51,
138-139
SAND, 118-119
SAND AND ROCK, 120-121
SAND DOLLAR, 122-123
SANDPIPER, 124-125
Sarah Elizabeth Hassell
Carmichael, 3
SCALLOP SHELL, 126-127
Sea Around Us, The, 24-25, 44-45
SEA GLASS, 128-129
sea levels, 92-93
sea turtle, 158-159
SEA WALL, 132-133
SEAGULLS, 130-131
seasons, 68-69
secure, 84-85
Sermon on the Mount, 116-117

Shaw, Luci, 22-23
shepherd, 96-97
Siena, Catherine of, 34-35
SIMPLICITY, 134-135
Sir Francis Drake, 30-31
Sir Walter Raleigh, 126-127
Skinner, Betty, 5
Smith, Huston, 6-7
Smith, Jennifer, 5
Smith, Joseph, 86-87
snorkel, 160-161
SOLITUDE, 136-137
solitude, 14-15
Spain, 126-127
spokes, 20-21
St. Aidan of Lindisfarne, 14-15
St. Augustine of Hippo, 88-89
St. Francis by the Sea Episcopal Church, 174-175
St. James' tomb, 126-127
star, 70-71
STARFISH, 138-139
STARS, 140-141
stars, 44-45
Statery, Cary, 5
STEADFAST LOVE, 142-143
Stevenson, Mary, 52-53
storm, 132-133
STORMS, 144-145
storms, 66-67
Sue Monk Kidd, 136-137
SUN, 146-147
SURFING, 148-149
Susanne Vanzant Hassell, 10, 191

T
T. S. Eliot, 176-177
tall ships, 56-57
Ten Boom, Corrie, 54-55
Teresa, Mother, 40-41
Tertullian, 46-47
thanks, 66-67
Thich Nhat Hanh, 6-7
thin places, 6-7
Thomas S. Monson, 86-87
Thomas, R.S., 8-9, 166-167
TIDEPOOL, 150-151
TIDES, 152-153

tides, 154-155
TIPS FOR THE JOURNEY, 8-9
todah, 66-67
tomb of St. James, 126-127
Tortoise and the Hare, 158-159
Tozer, A.W. , 148-149
Trevor Francis, 142-143
trials, 128-129, 160-161
TRUE SELF, 154-155
TRUST, 156-157
trust, 50-51, 114-115, 162-163
TURTLE, 158-159
turtles, 96-97
Tutu, Desmond, 138-139

U
Under the Sea Wind, 44-45
UNDERWATER SEA LIFE, 160-161

V
vanity, 58-59

W
WAITING, 162-163
WALKING, 164-165
walls, 132-133
Walter Raleigh, Sir, 126-127
WAVES, 166-167
WHALE, 168-169
wheel, 20-21
Whiting, Rev. William, 106-107
wideness of the sea, 88-89
wild geese, 60-61
William Blake, 118-119
wind and seas, 112-113
WIND AND WAVES, 170-171
wisdom, 170-171
WONDER, 172-173
Wonderstruck, 172-173
WORSHIP, 174-175

Y
yielding, 132-133

Z
Zinn, John Kabat, 148-149

COPYRIGHTS

Pages 34-35, Deep Water
Catherine of Siena, quote shared by Eileen Judice.

Pages 40-41, Drop in the Ocean
Mother Teresa quotation found in *Like a Drop in the Ocean: 99 Sayings by Mother Teresa* edited by W. Bader. Used by permission of New City Press.

Julia Carney, "Little Things."

Pages 44-45, Eternity
Under the Sea Wind, Penguin Group USA, New York, new editions 1996, 2007. *The Sea Around Us* by Rachael Carson.

Pages 50-51, Floating
Excerpt from *Earth Gospel: A Guide to Prayer for God's Creation* by Sam Hamilton-Poore. Copyright 2008. Used by permission from Upper Room Books. books.upperoom.org

"The Avowal" by Denise Levertov, from THE STREAM AND THE SAPPHIRE, copyright © 1984 by Denise Levertov. Reprinted by permission of New Directions Publishing Corp.

Pages 54-55, Forgiveness
Photo by iStock.com/Christine Gehrig.

Pages 56-57, Freedom
John Masefield, "Sea Fever", from *Saltwater Ballads*

Photo by Tandem/Matthew Kuhns

Pages 62-63, Generosity
John Bell, *He Was in the World: Meditations for Public Worship*.

Pages 64-65, God's Love
Frederick Martin Lehman, "The Love of God."

Pages 68-69, Grey Seas
Amy Charmichael, *His Thoughts Said, His Father Said*, Christian Literature Crusade, USA, 1941

John Claypool, *The Light Within You*, Word, 1983

Pages 74-75, Hermit Crab
Photo by iStock.com/Igor I. Byrko.

Pages 76-77, Heron
Patricia Lunetta, "The Visit".

Photo by Tandem/Ian Shive

Pages 80-81, Island
John Donne, "Meditation XVII" *Devotions Upon Emergent Occasions.*

Pages 82-83, Journey
Fiona Martin, "Columba's Bay".

Pages 84-85, Kelp
Photo by National Geographic Creative/Brian Skerry

Pages 86-87, Lighthouse
Henry Wadsworth Longfellow, "The Lighthouse"

Thomas S. Monson, Joseph Smith, Gorden B. Hinkley, *LDS Gems and Inspirational Quotes.*

Pages 88-89, Mercy
Frederick W. Faber, "There's a Wideness in God's Mercy"

Pages 90-91, Moon
Alexander Carmichael, *Carmina Gadelica*

Esther de Wall, *God Under My Roof: Celtic Songs and Blessings*

Pages 94-95, Night
J. Philip Newell, *Celtic Benediction: Morning and Night Prayer,* © 2000 Wm. B. Eerdmans Publishing Company, Grand Rapids, MI. Reprinted by permission of the publisher; all rights reserved.

Lucile H. Jones, *It's All Right to Cry*

Pages 96-97, Originality
Brian McLaren, *Generous Orthodoxy*

Photo by Tandem/Ian Shive

Mary Oliver, *Blue Pastures*

Pages 106-107, Peril on the Sea
Rev. William Whiting, "Eternal Father Strong to Save"

Pages 110-111, Prayer
Michael Casey, *Toward God*
Richard Foster, *Celebration of Discipline*

Pages 112-113, Protection
Henri Nouwen, *Discernment: Reading the Signs of Daily Life*

Pages 118-119, Sand
William Blake, "Auguries of Innocence"

Pages 120-121, Sand and Rock
Edward Mote, "On Christ the Solid Rock I Stand"

Pages 126-127, Scallop Shell
Photo by Kathy Kilgore Garvey

Pages 130-131, Seagulls
Whispers of His Power by Amy Carmichael, ©1982 by the Dohnavur Fellowship. Used by permission of CLC Publications. May not be further reproduced. All rights reserved.

Pages 134-135, Simplicity
Robert M. Hamma, *Earth's Echo* © 2002 by Sorin Books, a division of Ave Maria Press

Anne Morrow Lindbergh, *Gift from the Sea*

Pages 136-137, Solitude
Anne Morrow Lindbergh, *Gift from the Sea*

Sue Monk Kidd, *When the Heart Waits: Spiritual Direction for Life's Sacred Questions*

Pages 138-139, Starfish
He Was in the World: Meditations for Public Worship p.11, Wild Goose Publications, Iona Coummunity, Glasgow, Scotland, 1995.

Photo by Emily Huff

Pages 140-141, Stars
"Small Galaxy" from THE ORDERING OF LOVE: THE NEW AND COLLECTED POEMS OF MADELEINE L'ENGLE, copyright © 2005 by Crosswicks, Ltd. Used by permission of WaterBrook Multnomah, an imprint of the Crown Publishing Group, a division of Random House LLC. All rights reserved.

Pages 142-143, Steadfast Love
S.Trevor Francis, "Oh the Deep Deep Love of Jesus"

Pages 144-145, Storms
J.Philip Newell, *Celtic Benediction: Morning and Night Prayer,* © 2000 Wm. B. Eerdmans Publishing Company, Grand Rapids, MI. Reprinted by permission of the publisher; all rights reserved.

Pages 146-147, Sun
Brother Ramon, *Seven Days of Solitude*

Pages 148-149, Surfing
A.W. Tozer, *The Pursuit of God*

Photo by Tandem/Daniel Kuras

Pages 150-151, Tidepool
Eugene Peterson, *Conversations: The Message With Its Translator*

Pages 154-155, True Self
Joan Anderson, *A Year By The Sea*

Pages 156-157, Trust
Oceans (Where Feet May Fail) written by Joel Houston, Matt Crocker, Salomon Lighthelm. Copyright © 2013 Hillsong Music Publishing (APRA) (adm. In the US and Canada at CapitolCMGPublishing.com) All rights reserved. Used by permission. International Copyright Secured. All rights Reserved. Used by Permission.

Pages 158-159, Turtle
John Hay, *The Undiscovered Country*

Pages 164-165, Walking
"*I Go Down to the Shore*", from *A THOUSAND MORNINGS by Mary Oliver*, copyright © 2012 by Mary Oliver. Used by permission of The Penguin Press, a division of The Penguin Group (USA) LLC.

Kathleen Norris, *The Quotidian Mysteries*

Pages 166-167, Waves
R.S. Thomas, "The Other"

Pages 168-169, Whale
Herman Melville, *Moby Dick*

Photo by National Geographic Creative/Brian Skerry

Pages 172-173, Wonder
Margaret Feinberg, *Wonderstruck: Awaken to the Nearness of God*

Pages 174-175, Worship
Poem by Peter Makuck copyright © 2012. Used in Celtic Eucharist for St. Francis by the Sea Episcopal Church, Salter Path, NC.

Pages 176-177, End of Walk
T. S. Eliot, "Little Gidding", *Four Quartets*

Prayer from Commitment Service, *Iona Abbey Worship Book*, by the Iona Coummunity, Copyright © 2001, Wild Goose Resource Group, Iona Community, Scotland. GIA Publications Inc., exclusive North American agent, 7404 S. Mason Ave. Chicago, IL 60638. www.giamusic.com 800.442.1358. All rights reserved. Used by permission.

Scripture Quotations

The following Pilgrims generously shared their thoughts and ideas for this book.

14-15, Balance
Poem shared by Dr. David Gayk

18-19, Broken Seashells
Idea shared by Sami Parker

64-65, God's Love
Hymn shared by Nancy Vanzant Goodrum

72-73, Harbor
Quote shared by Debbie Henn

76-77, Heron
Shared by Emily Huff

92-93, Moon and Tides
Idea shared by Nancy Vanzant Goodrum

96-97, Opsreys
Story about the mother birds shared by Cary Slatery

150-151, Tidepool
Idea shared by Nancy Vanzant Goodrum

156-157, Trust
Song shared by Carrie Jo Pinckard

172-173, Wonder
Story about "pixie dust" shared by Emily Huff

174-175, Worship
Shared by Amanda Arwe

THE PILGRIMAGE CONTINUES...

Even as this book goes to press, we are discovering new gifts in nature. *Pilgrim Walk in the Woods* was published in 2011 and a third book in the series, *Pilgrim Walk in the City*, is expected in 2015.

We'd love to hear from you. If you make an interesting discovery, send us your reflection and we might include it in an upcoming book, or a future edition of *Pilgrim Walk in the Woods* or *Pilgrim Walk at the Sea*. To make a submission or suggestion for future editions, visit us at holypaths.org. Likewise, if you have enjoyed this book, additional copies of either Pilgrim Walk in the series may be purchased for friends at holypaths.org

All proceeds go to Holy Paths, Inc, a 501c3 non-profit committed to supporting communities of faith in their journey toward wholeness and intimacy with God. Susanne provides spiritual direction, an ancient discipline that involves careful listening and guidance for growing in faith. Holy Paths hosts contemplative retreats designed to provide rest from the demands of life and space to hear how God is leading. For more information, visit holypaths.org.

Holy Paths
GUIDANCE | COMPANIONSHIP | REST